LIVING THE MASS

LIVING
THE MASS

How One Hour a Week Can Change Your Life

FR. DOMINIC GRASSI *and* JOE PAPROCKI

LOYOLAPRESS.
A JESUIT MINISTRY
Chicago

LOYOLA PRESS.
A JESUIT MINISTRY

3441 N. Ashland Avenue
Chicago, Illinois 60657
(800) 621-1008
www.loyolapress.com

In accordance with c. 827, permission to publish is granted on May 31, 2011 by Rev. Msgr. John F. Canary, Vicar General of the Archdiocese of Chicago. Permission to publish is an official declaration of ecclesiastical authority that the material is free from doctrinal and moral error. No legal responsibility is assumed by the grant of this permission.

Cover photos, top: iStockphoto.com/ooyoo; bottom: Zvonimir Atletic/Shutterstock.com Interior design by Arc Group Ltd.

Library of Congress Cataloging-in-Publication Data
Grassi, Dominic.
  Living the Mass : how one hour a week can change your life / Dominic Grassi and Joe Paprocki—[Revision].
    p. cm.
  ISBN-13: 978-0-8294-3614-3
  ISBN-10: 0-8294-3614-6
  1. Mass I. Paprocki, Joe. II. Title.
  BX2230.3.G72 2011
  264'.02036—dc22

                                              2011018498

Printed in the United States of America
  14 15 16 Bang 10 9 8 7 6 5

We dedicate this book to the late Rev. Jack Daley.
For Joe, he was a godfather to his son Mike.
For Dominic, he was a classmate in the seminary.
For both, he was a priest, confidant,
role model, and dear friend.

Contents

Acknowledgments

Thanks to: Joe Durepos and Steve Connor for urging Dom and me to undertake this revision; Dom, for such wonderful collaboration and for a long-lasting friendship; D. Todd Williamson for his friendship, liturgical expertise, and great lunches in Greek Town; Denyse Wang for a superb job of organizing information on the 3rd Edition of the Roman Missal; and most of all to Joanne, Mike, and Amy, who fill my life and make me whole. (JSP)

Thanks to the people of St. Josaphat and St. Gertrude parishes in Chicago, with whom I have been privileged to worship and where faith allows me to grow in appreciation and love of the Mass. Reconnecting with Joe and collaborating with him continue to be a grace in my life. (DJG)

We would like to thank all the fine people of Loyola Press for offering us this opportunity to share our thoughts about how the Mass challenges, compels, and energizes us to practice our faith.

Above all, as we voice appreciation for all the sources of inspiration for this book, we take our cue from the last words spoken in the Mass: "Thanks be to God!" (DJG and JSP)

Introduction

Reconnecting Mass and Daily Living

How would you like to meet God? What if you had the opportunity to encounter God in a very real and personal way each and every week and build a relationship with him that would carry you through the other six days of the week? That opportunity exists, and you are invited. It's called the Mass.

Perhaps you've never thought of the Mass as a life-changing event. When you stop to think of it, however, how could an encounter with the Creator of the universe *not* be life-changing? We, as Catholics, believe that the Mass is God's most profound way of entering into the lives of his people. It can and should make a difference. So why do only 25–35 percent of Catholics actually attend Sunday Mass? People give various reasons, blaming their disinterest on everything from the changes that followed the Second Vatican Council and the more recent sex-abuse scandal to poor music and weak preaching. These and other factors have played a role in some Catholics' decisions to stop attending Mass.

We propose another reason. Too many of us Catholics do not understand our baptism; we think that our baptism was a once-and-done event as opposed to something we are called to practice each and every day. Think about it. If someone asks you, "Are you a practicing Catholic?" chances are, you will answer based on whether or not you attend Mass on Sunday. Now, let's rephrase that question.

Are you practicing your baptism?

This question seems a lot harder to answer, doesn't it? Taking the time to go to Mass is one issue. Waking up each day to practice our baptism is another. In fact, going to Mass on Sunday makes little sense unless we understand it within the context of how we live the other six days of the week. The reason we go to Mass in the first place is because, through our baptism, we have made a commitment to something and to someone. If we truly understood what it means to practice our baptism, we would see more clearly that participating fully, consciously, and actively in Sunday Mass is an integral and necessary part of the ongoing and life-changing experience of following Jesus Christ.

What we Catholics need is a solid connection between what we believe, how we worship, and how we live our faith on a daily basis. Making the Mass more meaningful is not simply about improving the quality of the music played, the homily preached, or the manner in which the altar is decorated (although improvement in these areas is often sorely needed!). Rather, the solution lies in growing in our understanding of God's connection to our daily lives and how the Mass invites and challenges us to practice our baptism on a daily basis. The solution lies in recognizing that baptism is a commitment to a way of life that needs to be sustained and nourished by celebration of the Eucharist.

This is not just another book that explains the parts of the Mass. There are already dozens of those available. This is a book that challenges us to look at our own way of life. It is a book about how one hour on Sunday morning can and should shape how we "live and move and have our being" (Acts 17:28) the other 167 hours of the week. It is a book about obligation: not just our obligation to go to church on Sunday but our obligation to live the Catholic way of life that we committed to in baptism, a sacrament of initiation that reaches completion in the celebration of the Eucharist. Our goal is to show that the Mass is not something we attend but something we do and something that prepares us to "go forth" and do what Jesus asks of us.

Do This in Memory of Me: Do *What*?

When we hear "Do this in memory of me" at Mass, we are being reminded that Jesus is telling us to do much more than to go to Mass on Sundays. He is inviting us to choose a way of life that embraces the same selfless love he showed for us. It is this way of life that we have chosen in baptism. One of the main reasons we often don't know what the Mass is sending us out to do is that we don't understand what we promised to do in our baptism in the first place. When we made a commitment to become part of Jesus' church (a commitment that was made for us by those who loved us and wanted the best for us if we were baptized as infants), we began the process of being initiated into a way of life. It is no coincidence that in the very early church, members of the church were said to belong to "the Way" (Acts 9:2; 19:9, 23; 22:4; 24:14, 22).

Just what does this way of life call us to do? The answer lies in the words used in the rite of baptism as the priest or deacon anoints with oil:

> God, the Father of our Lord Jesus Christ . . .
> now anoints you with the chrism of salvation. As
> Christ was anointed *priest, prophet,* and *king,* so
> may you live always as a member of his body, shar-
> ing everlasting life. [emphasis added]

As disciples of Christ, we are called to love and serve God and others by sharing in Jesus' ministry as priest, prophet, and king. This means that in our daily living we are called to do the following:

- As priest: make Jesus present to others; praise and worship God through our lives; offer ourselves and our lives in sacrifice; help others gain access to God; intercede for the needs of the world and act as part of God's response to those needs; help others find God through us.

- As prophet: speak on behalf of the oppressed; clearly and boldly speak God's word; bear witness, evangelize and catechize; bring hope to those in despair; challenge people and institutions to be faithful; fearlessly speak out about injustice.

- As king: serve and protect the vulnerable; provide for those unable to provide for themselves; love enemies; lay down our lives for others; work for justice; live with dignity; respect others' dignity; restore lives that are broken; represent God's will; protect our world and all of God's creation.

At the end of Mass, when the priest or deacon says, "Go in peace," he is sending us forth on a mission to share in Jesus' ministry as priest, prophet, and king. If we understand that this is our calling, our mandate, then we will better understand what it is we are doing and celebrating at Mass and how the Mass prepares, enables, challenges, and inspires us to go forth and do just that.

While Sunday, our Sabbath, is held traditionally as a day of rest, the word *liturgy*, which comes from the Greek word *leitourgia*, means "the work of the people." The liturgy is indeed "work," or something that we do. At the same time, the doing comes not only during that one hour in church but even more so when we leave the church building and go forth into daily life. Come Monday morning, with our batteries recharged, we are now ready to forge ahead and attempt to put into practice what we began working on at Mass: a commitment to go forth, living out our baptismal calling and doing the work of discipleship.

In this book, we will identify and describe what Christians are called to do and be; what qualities and skills are needed to live as Christians; and how the one hour a week we spend at Mass can, should, and will change our lives.

One More Note

Much has been made of the implementation of the translation of the 3rd Edition of the Roman Missal during Advent, 2011. The fact is, these changes in some of the words that we use at Mass have provided a natural opportunity to step back and examine what we do at Mass and how that is connected with daily life. Although this book incorporates the changes from the 3rd Edition of the Roman Missal, it is not a book about those changes per se. Rather, this book will enable you to reflect on the Mass as a whole, pondering the words and actions of the Mass that express our faith while transforming us. Actions are often preceded by, and inspired by, words. The "doing" of our faith is inspired by the words we pray at Mass. The better we understand the words, signs, and symbols of the liturgy, the better able we will be to live the Mass each day. What the Mass is, what Jesus gave us—the gift of himself—will never change.

Beginning with the End in Mind

Thanks Be to God

In my book *Bumping into God in the Kitchen*, I include my mother's recipe for fried egg balls. I always wanted to be able to make them the way she did. But every time I tried, I failed. Instead of the round and golden delicacy I remembered, mine turned out flat and oily. Finally, I called her and asked her what I might have done wrong. Patiently, she asked me to list all the ingredients I'd been using. When I read my list, she laughed. I had left out the baking soda. When I asked how much I should use, she replied cryptically that I would find out. Figuring that using none had caused a failure, it made sense to me that a little would be good—but using a lot of it would be even better! So I liberally added the baking soda to the batter, and I do mean liberally. The batter swelled up into a soggy and inedible concoction that looked more like a football than the petite egg balls I used to enjoy. The next time, I used a little less, and it was better. I kept experimenting until I got it just the way I wanted it, looking and tasting like mom's—and now my own—egg ball. I had known what the end product should look like, but I had no clear idea of how to get there! (DJG)

In his book *The 7 Habits of Highly Effective People,* Stephen Covey identifies one of the seven habits as "begin with the end in mind." He asserts that "to begin with the end in mind means to start with a clear understanding of your destination. It means to know where you're going so that you better understand where you are now and so that the steps you take are always in the right direction" (p. 98). Any cook will tell you that this is the key to following a recipe and ending up with a creation that will wow the taste buds. Following this sound advice, we're going to begin our exploration of the Mass, not with the Introductory Rites, but with a quick peek at the end of the Mass, so that we, too, will have a clearer understanding of our destination and the steps we need to take to reach it.

It's no coincidence that the word *Mass* comes from the Concluding Rites of the liturgy. In Latin, the words of the dismissal are *Ite! Missa est!* meaning, "Go! You are dismissed!" It is from this word *missa* that we have the word *Mass.* We indeed begin with the end in mind. We are sent forth at the end of the Mass with any one of the following formulas:

- "Go forth, the Mass is ended."

- "Go and announce the Gospel of the Lord."

- "Go in peace, glorifying the Lord by your life."

- "Go in peace."

And our response is, "Thanks be to God."

Whatever formula is used, the message is the same: We gotta go! Can't stay! We are being given marching orders. The key to understanding, and thus living, the Mass is found in these words with which the Mass ends. So, beginning with the end in mind, let's explore how the Concluding Rites of the Mass shed light on our destination and on how the parts of the Mass serve to send us in the right direction.

What Does Baptism Call Us to Do?

At the end of the Mass, the priest or deacon says, "Go in peace." It is very clear that we are being sent forth to do something! We are being sent forth to do the things that Jesus does. In fact, Jesus is all about doing. Throughout the Gospels, Jesus emphasizes over and over again that to be his disciple means to *do*.

- "In everything do to others as you would have them do to you" (Matthew 7:12).

- "Not everyone who says to me, 'Lord, Lord,' will enter the kingdom of heaven, but only one who does the will of my Father in heaven" (Matthew 7:21).

- "Truly I tell you, just as you did not do it to one of the least of these, you did not do it to me" (Matthew 25:45).

- "Whoever does the will of God is my brother and sister and mother" (Mark 3:35).

- "Love your enemies, do good to those who hate you" (Luke 6:27).

- "Why do you call me 'Lord, Lord,' and do not do what I tell you?" (Luke 6:46).

- "Very truly, I tell you, the one who believes in me will also do the works that I do and, in fact, will do greater works than these" (John 14:12).

- "You are my friends if you do what I command you" (John 15:14).

Most important, at the Last Supper—where Jesus instituted the Eucharist—Jesus got up from the table and washed the feet of his apostles saying, "You also should do as I have done to you" (John 13:15). The message, though not immediately clear to St. Peter, is clear to us: To be a follower of Jesus means to be a doer. We just need to hear the word *go!*

And so, indeed, we are told to "go" as the Mass ends. While we may remain for a while after Mass to share some hospitality, we are directed to leave. Our work here is done. We were not baptized in order to spend all our time in church. Rather, the responsibilities that we agreed to take on as members of the church must continue in the world outside the church doors. It is the task of the laity in the congregation to take what just happened with them in order to reveal God's presence in the world. That world is everywhere, including our homes, neighborhoods, communities, and workplaces. "Go" means leaving the safety and security of the sanctuary. It means internalizing the word of God and going forth to proclaim it, both in word and deed, to others who may not be as receptive to hearing or experiencing it. "Go," we are urged. It is the only way that Jesus Christ will reach those who have not joined us in worship and in prayer. Too many choose not to worship with us, so we must go to them instead of waiting for them to come to us.

But we are not simply dismissed haphazardly. We are told to "go *in peace*" (emphasis added). We are told to go with that which we have received and shared with our fellow Mass-goers: the peace of our Lord Jesus Christ. What does it mean to "go in peace"? Well, obviously, we are not at peace if we are fighting one another. There is no peace if we are distracted by hateful thoughts. We cannot find the peace we are to leave with if we are angry, bitter, distrustful, or, worst of all, judgmental. The Mass calls us to begin by being at peace with ourselves. While we have our faults and our sinfulness, the Mass invites us to place them all before our loving God who is only too happy to grant us peace. The Mass invites us to let go of our sins and the accompanying guilt so that we can be at peace.

Being at peace does not mean that we leave church worry free. Rather, we come to accept whatever doubts remain even after the celebration is over. We remember that there can be no real faith without doubt. *Peace* does not translate into the absence of all problems or into certainty about all matters. False certainty leads to arrogance, which often leads to our judgmental attitude toward anyone who does not agree with us. This, of course, does not lead to peace but to harm.

To "go in peace" means more than just being at peace with ourselves. The Mass sends us forth to "go in peace" with others as well. By walking in peace, we necessarily share that peace with others, for being at peace with ourselves makes it infinitely easier to be at peace with others. The word of God that is proclaimed to us at Mass challenges us to leave behind anything that separates us from one another: jealousy, bitterness, and prejudices. Even though we may enter the church building with these burdens, we are called to turn them over to the Lord and not pick them up as we leave. To "go in peace" means that we leave with a noticeable change in ourselves. Where the world attempts to drive wedges between us and our neighbors, the Mass sends us out to bring reconciliation to those whose lives are broken and chaotic. We are sent to live in peace with one another, as manifested in our words and responses, in our offers to help others, in all our actions, and where it cannot be seen—our attitudes and feelings, thoughts and desires. We are called to bring peace to all of God's creation.

> When my daughter Amy was about five years old, she asked me, as we were leaving church one Sunday, "When can *I* get some peace?" My wife and I weren't quite sure what she was talking about, so we asked her to explain what she meant. She said, "When you go up to the priest and he gives you peace . . . when can I get some, too?" She was referring to Holy Communion. Like all children at that age, they want to be a part of what the grown-ups are doing. She saw us going up to the priest to "get" something. To her, that something was "peace." She heard, "The peace of the Lord be with you always," and "Let us offer one another a sign of peace," and "Grant us peace," and, of course, "Go in peace." She concluded that this "peace" that was being spoken of was what we were being given when we came forward

for Holy Communion. In essence, she was right. When we receive the body and blood of Jesus, we open our hearts to the real presence of Jesus, the Prince of Peace. Amy understood at a very young age what the words of a famous bumper sticker are trying to communicate: "No Jesus, No Peace. Know Jesus, Know Peace." (JSP)

The words *Go in peace* are not just nice words to nod our heads to because we agree with them in theory. To literally "go in peace" is an incredible challenge. As we reflect on what these words mean, we begin to realize just how transforming the Mass is supposed to be. We begin to see that because of our baptism as Christians, we are called to be different. We are called to be holy—in the words of Peter's epistle, a people "set apart." We begin to realize that to "go in peace" means much more than to leave with a good feeling. It means that we leave church with the intention of making peace happen in our personal lives and in what happens around us.

The Mass directs us to "go in peace, glorifying the Lord by your life." We are not just humanists who feel compelled to be nice to our brothers and sisters only. The peacemaking we do is in the name of the Lord. Our Lord is not some remote or punishing God, nor is he some pantheistic deity who is hiding in the bushes somewhere. Jesus Christ became flesh, lived among us, died for our sins, rose from the dead, and opens the gates of heaven for all of us. In the creed, we proudly proclaim our faith in a triune God—God who creates us, God who lived among us and redeems us, and God whom we experience in the depth of our being. This is the God we love and serve and take with us when we leave church. This is the God in whose name we are sent.

God's very nature is relational, and so we find ourselves in relationship with God. That is why we are told to go in peace, glorifying the Lord by our lives. The best way to glorify God is through not only words but also deeds. We all know that love is more than just words; it moves into actions. The Mass urges us to love God by acting against injustice, violence, war, prejudice—anything and everything that gets in the way of our loving one another. We must also do the small, everyday things that strengthen our relationships with those around us. And we are also responsible to act as part of the human family. On a global level our love calls us to fulfill responsibilities that we cannot ignore. We go forth to share in Jesus' priestly ministry, making Jesus present to the world. We go forth to share in Jesus' ministry as prophet, speaking on behalf of the oppressed and bringing hope to those in despair. We go forth to share in Jesus' ministry as king, serving and protecting the vulnerable who inhabit our world and providing for the needs of others, and indeed, the needs of all creation. We go forth recognizing that Jesus is present not only under the appearance of bread and wine but also in "the poor, the sick, and the imprisoned" (*Catechism of the Catholic Church*, 1373).

And finally, we are told to "glorify the Lord with our lives." We do that best by serving others. It's not about us. We cannot leave church with our own agendas, expecting to do things our own way. We serve and glorify our God and not ourselves. It must be God's path we take, God's words we speak, and God's actions we perform. It must be God's will that is done. After all, shortly before communion we prayed, "thy will be done" in the Lord's Prayer. We are sent forth, with God's blessing, to do God's bidding. Again, this is not an easy task, because to glorify the Lord with our lives means to serve our neighbors. To glorify the Lord with our lives is something we do, not only in church, but primarily in our homes, neighborhoods, and workplaces. To make matters more challenging, God's will quite often runs counter to our human instincts, no matter how noble we might think them to be. God's will can also be maddeningly mysterious. This is where faith comes in. It takes faith to glorify the Lord through service. It takes great faith to respond in a way counter to what others expect, in a way that seems to isolate us, making us look different or strange. In those times of painful loneliness we need to remember that we are not alone. The Mass strengthens our faith by bringing us into communion with Jesus and our brothers and sisters. Jesus Christ, whom we took into our hearts and souls in the Eucharist, walks with us. And all those with whom we shared a sign of Christ's peace are fighting the same battle, struggling in the same way. The Mass helps us overcome isolation and empowers us to recognize that so many others, because of their faith, are in the fight with us. And "If God is for us, who is against us?" (Romans 8:31). We will never be alone.

Given all the above, when we are sent forth to "go in peace," our only response must be a resounding "Thanks be to God." When we say these words, we are doing more than thanking God for what we have experienced in the past hour or so. Likewise, we are not thanking God that Mass is over, as relieved parents of a two-year-old who just made it through the liturgy with Cheerios, picture books, and a minimum of trips to the bathroom might be inclined to do. When we say, "Thanks be to God," we are thanking

God for the faith that brought us to the Mass and for all those with whom we have shared that faith: from the saints to our deceased loved ones, all of whom we have remembered in the Mass. For two thousand years, people of faith have gathered to celebrate the Eucharist. We continue to do so today, united with them all.

Most important, when we say, "Thanks be to God," we are showing gratitude for the trust that God places in us to be Christ's loving presence in the world. We call ourselves Christians. Christ lives and works in and through us, the people of God. We are happy to be called to the Supper of the Lamb, which prepares us to "go in peace." When we say, "Thanks be to God," we are thanking God profoundly and joyfully that the Mass is over and that we can leave church with a renewed commitment to make God's love and peace real in our individual circles of influence. It's as if we are runners at the starting line after months of training, waiting for the race to finally begin. Everything has led up to this moment. Now we will give it our best effort. We'll see what we can do, and we'll be ready for whatever comes our way. God has freed us from serving other "masters" that we have allowed into our lives. We are free to do what we were truly created to do: glorify the Lord through lives of loving and serving others.

With the end of the Mass in mind, we are able to go back now to the beginning of the Mass and start as we, the community of faith, enter the church—be it a cathedral in Europe, a shed in some mission land, or our local parish—and begin the celebration of the Eucharist, our sacred liturgy.

■ ■ ■

The world wants peace; the world needs peace. Peace is not a utopia, nor an inaccessible ideal, nor an unrealizable dream. Peace is possible. And because it is possible, peace is our duty: our grave duty, our supreme responsibility.

Blessed Pope John Paul II
Message to the United Nations Special Session
June 11, 1982

2

From Individuals to Community

The Introductory Rites

I found myself standing in line at the Holy Thursday pot-luck dinner next to Joan, a middle-aged schoolteacher who had never married. In the course of our conversation, I commented about the parish's idea of offering a simple tuna casserole dinner for Good Friday. Without hesitation, she replied, "Oh good! I get to eat with other people two days in a row!" It had never occurred to me that a number of people like Joan ate their meals alone every day. Having grown up in a family of nine children and then spending every day with my wife and two children, I rarely had to eat alone. I got to thinking about how much effort many of us put into being alone, being separated, and being individuals. We put on headphones to block out the world and have TVs in every room so we can enjoy our time alone. We hope that no one sits next to us on the train or in the movie theater so that we can enjoy some space to ourselves. We go to great lengths to avoid contact with other people.

We have to be careful about what we wish for. We just might get it. (JSP)

When we "go in peace," we go not as "lone rangers" but as members of a community. We go with a sense of belonging. We go with a sense of selflessness and of hospitality. We go with eyes that recognize others as brothers and sisters, not strangers or competitors. How do we get to this point? The fact is, from the moment we enter the church for the celebration of the Mass, we are invited or, better yet, challenged, to leave our individualism behind, which is something we're not used to doing.

In and of itself, individualism is not a bad thing. Individualism left unchecked, however, breeds narcissism. Solitude is a valued necessity. Narcissism is a debilitating self-centeredness. While narcissism is a personality disorder, it is also a societal condition. Day after day, we are bombarded with messages from many sources that encourage us to pursue our own gratification. Whether we are aware of it or not, we tend toward self-obsession to the exclusion of others. It leads to the isolation that is sin.

A narcissistic attitude was the downfall of Adam and Eve. Obsessive self-centeredness was the temptation of the serpent, who said, in essence, "Don't worry about God or anyone else—think of yourself!" Jesus himself was tempted in the desert to look out for his own needs instead of the needs of others. And again, in Gethsemane, Jesus was tempted to live according to the credo "my will be done" rather than "thy will be done." Narcissistic attitudes, a form of idolatry, tempt us to offer our allegiances to a variety of things that we think will bring us gratification. No matter what, narcissism by its very nature is doomed to fail.

The Mass is a remedy for the narcissism that pervades our society.

Beginning with the Introductory Rites of the Mass, each of us is invited and challenged to enter a community and to accept the reality that "it's not about me." Whereas we tend to run past one another anonymously on our way in and out of train stations, airports, supermarkets, and malls, we enter church by greeting and being greeted, even if we are strangers to one another. We are met by a hospitality that says, *You are not here alone. You are part of a community.* This hospitality teaches us that our dignity comes not from being an individual but from being in relationship as brothers and sisters to one another.

The Introductory Rites of the Mass are sometimes referred to as the gathering rites. This gathering, however, takes place on two levels. On one level, there is a gathering of individuals into community. *The General Instruction of the Roman Missal* (2010) tells us that "at Mass or the Lord's Supper the People of God is called together" (27). It goes on to say that "in the celebration of the Mass . . . Christ is really present in the very assembly gathered in his name" (27). The Mass is a "communitarian" prayer, not a private devotion. Our participation in singing, in the dialogues between the priest and the people, in our acclamations, gestures, responses, postures, and even in shared silence are "not simply outward signs of communal celebration but foster and bring about communion between Priest and people" (34). In essence, the Introductory Rites of the Mass tell us that we cannot hope to recognize Jesus' presence in the bread and wine if we don't first begin to recognize his presence in those gathered around us as we prepare to celebrate.

> Bruce is a deacon at St. Ailbe Parish in Chicago, a middle-class African American community. I taught Bruce when he was in the deacon program. Likewise, I had taught several other people from St. Ailbe in various lay ministry and catechist formation classes. I ran into Bruce one day, and he invited me to bring my family to St. Ailbe for Mass. A few months later, I took him up on the offer and persuaded my wife and kids to attend with me. They no doubt felt some discomfort over the notion of going to a church where they didn't know anyone. No sooner did we walk into the church at St. Ailbe than Bruce came running up and threw his arms around me to welcome me to the parish. He then proceeded to do the same with my wife and kids, whom he had never met. They were dumbfounded that a "stranger" could be so welcoming. Better yet, they were genuinely tickled! Before another moment passed, the pastor, Fr. John, came dashing through the foyer and stopped to greet each of us in the same manner, bear hugs and all. Ten or twenty feet later, I ran into several of the people whom I taught in lay-ministry and catechist formation classes. More hugs. As we headed to our pew, one of my wife's students from the Catholic high school at which she taught came over to greet her with a hug. Before we got to our seats, we had greeted and been greeted and hugged by at least a dozen people. Later, on the ride home, we all commented on how ironic it was that we were greeted with

more warmth at a parish we were visiting than we were ever greeted with at our home parish, where we can often slip in and slip out practically unnoticed. (JSP)

As mentioned before, gathering occurs on two levels. On one, we gather to form community. Some churches, like St. Ailbe, have come to recognize that such gathering is more than a simple nicety; it is a hallmark of discipleship. However, on another level, there is a gathering *within* ourselves that must also take place. When we arrive at church for Mass, we need some time to gather our thoughts, our wits, and ourselves. At the parish where my wife and I usually attend, a commentator welcomes the assembly, reads the announcements for that week, and then says, "Let us take a moment to center ourselves and to remind ourselves that we are in God's presence." For the next sixty to ninety seconds, there is silence until the opening hymn begins—a silence that enables us to gather within as we gather together as a community. In order for this type of gathering to take place, it is important to arrive at church early, first to have some time to be greeted and to greet neighbors, but then to sit or kneel in silent reflection. This allows us to more clearly connect with our thoughts and begin the process of refocusing our attention away from ourselves and onto God and our brothers and sisters. The purpose of the Introductory Rites is not only to bring individuals together to establish communion but also to predispose ourselves to listen to God's word actively and to celebrate the Eucharist worthily. Unless we take the time to do this, we remain wrapped up in our own concerns. Unless we take a few moments to gather ourselves, we run the risk of retaining a narcissistic attitude: obsessed with ourselves to the exclusion of others.

The various parts of the Introductory Rites help us begin this transformation. After we have settled in our places and given some silent time to gathering ourselves within, we are formally greeted and invited to turn our thoughts to the mystery of the feast or liturgical season we are celebrating. This is done either through an entrance chant or a brief introduction read by a commentator. Typically, the entrance chant is accomplished through "a suitable liturgical song." Unfortunately, some of us refrain from singing at Mass. We think that since we don't have a voice like a famous tenor or soprano, we should keep our mouths shut. The result, however, is that we end up separating ourselves from the larger community. We mistakenly think that by singing we may draw attention to ourselves when, by not singing, we are in fact keeping attention focused on ourselves. We would never dream of attending a birthday party and not joining in the singing of "Happy Birthday." Singing helps us gather with our brothers and sisters. By uniting our voices, we begin the process of uniting our hearts. Singing also helps us gather ourselves since the words of the hymns invite us to focus on the works of God for which we have gathered to give thanks. Singing warms us up and opens us up to all that God is offering us.

The entrance procession also helps us gather as a community. A good way to understand the entrance procession is to compare it to a parade. For most people, a parade is something to watch. Most of us don't get to actually walk in the parade, but we participate by watching from the side-lines and cheering for those in the parade. Why? Because most parades celebrate a victory. Parades find their roots in military conquests. When a triumphant army returned to its homeland, they would march, as if recreating the battle they had just won, giving everyone an opportunity to participate in a march toward victory. At the front of the parade would be the standard bearer, proudly proclaiming the identity of the victors.

In essence, the opening procession at Mass is a holy parade, a victory march. We may not all get to walk in the procession, but each of us—by virtue of our presence, our attention, and our participation in the triumphant song that accompanies the procession—gets to be a part of this march to victory. At the front of our holy parade is our standard bearer, the cross bearer, holding the symbol that defines who we are: followers of Jesus Christ. And just as a trophy is hoisted for all to see when a city hosts a victory, the cross stands as our trophy, God's trophy, symbolizing his victory over sin and death. Watch the fans in the city that brings home the Stanley Cup, the National Hockey League championship trophy. They not only cheer it, they also strain to touch it, even kiss it, as it is paraded through the city. How do you feel when the victorious cross is carried up the aisle at Mass? The opening procession is the victory march of the Mass.

In our daily lives, living the Mass means that we are to live each day as a victorious people, not because we ourselves have done anything to claim victory, but because we are loved by a God who has defeated sin and death and wishes to share that victory with us through his great mercy.

The cross, held high by an altar server, leads the procession and invites us to focus on Jesus' selfless act of love. The candles, also held by altar servers, light our way so that we can recognize the presence of Jesus in our midst and in those gathered with us. The book of the Gospels carried reverently by a lector or deacon reminds us to clear our minds so that we truly can be receptive to God's word. The priest, as the leader of the assembly, symbolizes the unity of all gathered in the name of Christ. The slow movement of the procession toward the sanctuary reminds us that we are all on this journey together, moving toward the Lord. When the priest and ministers bow to the altar and the priest and deacon kiss the altar, we are reminded that we have gathered around one table. Unlike a restaurant, where we can get our own private booths, this meal—more like a banquet—calls us to gather around one table. When all are in place and we have finished singing, the priest and everyone gathered make the sign of the cross by using the right hand to trace a cross from the forehead ("In the name of the Father . . .") down to the breastbone ("and of the Son . . .") and then from the left shoulder to the right shoulder ("and of the Holy Spirit. Amen"). This ancient Christian gesture reminds the baptized that we are sealed in Christ—we belong to him—and that we are to do all things in God's name.

> Priest: In the name of the Father, and of the Son,
>   and of the Holy Spirit.
> People: Amen.
> Priest: The grace of our Lord Jesus Christ,
> and the love of God,
> and the communion of the Holy Spirit
> be with you all.
> People: And with your spirit.

We do not gather in our own name; we gather "in the name of the Father, and of the Son, and of the Holy Spirit." The priest then extends a formal greeting to everyone present. Whereas we exchanged pleasantries and small talk with people before Mass, now we are greeted in ritual language, using words that have been used by the church since St. Paul first used them in a letter to greet the faith community at Corinth (see 2 Corinthians 13:13). This ritual language, rather than being stuffy or rigid, helps us realize that we are part of something bigger than ourselves.

This ritual greeting is much more than a way of saying hi! It is actually more of a wish than a greeting. In this respect, it can be compared to someone's saying, "May the Force be with you" in the movie *Star Wars*. These words were offered whenever someone was about to take on a profound and difficult task. In the same way, our exchange with the priest, "The Lord be with you. **And with your spirit**," represents our wish and the wish of the priest that we be filled with the grace we need as we undertake this profound task of celebrating the Mass. In addition, we will share this exchange three more times during the Mass: as we prepare to hear the Gospel, as we enter into the Eucharistic Prayer, and as we prepare to leave. At each of these moments, we stand on the threshold of a profound task for which we need God's grace.

In addition, by relying on the universal language of ritual words—words that other believers in other places are sharing—the priest is shunning any temptation to make himself the focus of attention, a temptation that comes when anyone is handed a microphone! By greeting the assembly in this manner, the priest is inviting each person to enter together into the ritual of the Mass, a ritual that shapes us and converts us into community.

At first glance, we may think that the priest is drawing attention to himself by wearing special clothing, called vestments. The intent of the ritual vestments, however, is quite the opposite. The vestments, in fact, cover the priest's individual identity and emphasize his role as priest of the gathered community. The purpose of the vestments is to conceal the priest's individuality and to draw the congregation's attention toward Christ, in whose name he serves. As the leader of the assembly, the priest is reminding us that, in baptism, each of us was given a garment to wear as a symbol of "putting on Christ." Although we do not wear this outer garment to Mass, each time we enter church and dip our fingers into the holy water, we remind ourselves that we must decrease and Jesus must increase.

The Introductory Rites of the Mass begin a process of conversion. By accepting and extending hospitality; by taking the time to gather ourselves; by joining voices in song; by observing the procession that symbolizes our communal faith journey; by recognizing that we gather around one table; by beginning, not in our own name but in the name of the Holy Trinity; and by being greeted and greeting the priest with ritual language, we have opened the door to a change of heart and mind. We are called to this weekly conversion, which invites us to shift attention away from ourselves and toward others. We become aware that we are not alone but are sharing this time and space with others. As this process unfolds, we become aware that our narcissistic attitudes may have hurt others; if our attention and focus are on ourselves, we run the risk of failing to recognize the presence of God in others. It is no coincidence that, immediately after greeting and being greeted, the Mass invites us to turn our attention to our need for forgiveness.

The Other Six Days of the Week

With regard to daily life, the Introductory Rites of the Mass invite and challenge us to

- take time on a daily basis to prayerfully gather ourselves;

- extend hospitality to those we encounter at work, on the street, and in our homes and communities;

- safeguard our need for solitude and privacy while remaining vigilant against the temptation to be individualistic;

- recognize the dignity of others, who are created in the image of God;

- invite others to walk with us on our journey, and offer to walk with others on theirs;

- overcome narcissistic attitudes and focus on the needs of others;

- seek out those who are alone (especially for meals) and offer our company.

■ ■ ■

For just as the body is one and has many members, and all the members of the body, though many, are one body, so it is with Christ. For in the one Spirit we were all baptized into one body—Jews or Greeks, slaves or free— and we were all made to drink of one Spirit.

Indeed, the body does not consist of one member but of many. If the foot were to say, "Because I am not a hand, I do not belong to the body," that would not make it any less a part of the body. And if the ear were to say, "Because I am not an eye, I do not belong to the body," that would not make it any less a part of the body. If the whole body were an eye, where would the hearing be? If the whole body were hearing, where would the sense of smell be? But as it is, God arranged the members in the body, each one of them, as he chose. If all were a single member, where would the body be? As it is, there are many members, yet one body. The eye cannot say to the hand, "I have no need of you," nor again the head to the feet, "I have no need of you."

1 Corinthians 12:12–21

3

A Healthy Dose of Humility

The Penitential Act

As a high school freshman, I was cursed with an over-abundance of "mouth" and, unfortunately, a severe lack of common sense. So when I caused a classmate to cry because of my unrelenting taunting—I had taken to calling him the "king of teachers' pets" because the gym teacher drove him to and from school every day— it is no wonder that one Friday afternoon the teacher told me to report to the physical-education office the following Monday morning. Realizing that I had really messed up, I searched my mind frantically to find the best way to cover myself. Should I deny everything? Place the blame on someone else? Say it was all done in good fun? I feverishly brainstormed ways to extricate myself from the mess I had created. I felt doubly awful when I found out that the coach was picking up this young man at an orphanage and driving him back there after school because he had no other way of making it to and from school. Dreading the arrival of Monday morning and desperately in need of support, I went to my three older brothers for advice. After they forced me to admit what a jerk I was, they gave me both the advice and the support that I truly needed. They told me to walk into the coach's office and, before he could say anything that we both might regret, look him directly in the eyes and say the following five things: I was wrong; there was no excuse for what I had done; I deserved whatever punishment he would give to me; I would make it up both to him and to the student that I hurt; it would never happen again. I was then to put my head down and not say another word until the coach was done with me. No excuses. No pleading. I was simply to place myself at his mercy. No matter what he said to me, I was to thank him and then walk out. I decided that I had no choice but to follow my brothers' advice to the letter. My brothers were right. The coach chose not to berate me. He did express his disappointment in me and told me that I had a lot to learn. Four years later, at graduation, he admitted to me that he had been ready to have me expelled. But my penitential attitude caught him completely off guard, so much so that he had forgotten even to give me a single detention. It is amazing what life-altering and humbling effects a sincere apology can have. (DJG)

When we "go in peace," we go with a sense of humility. We go having been "put in our place"—reminded of our own frailty and aware of God's great mercy, which strengthens us. We go not with a holier-than-thou attitude but with the realization that we are sinners, healed by the mercy of God. We go, warts and all, eager to share God's mercy with a broken world. How do we get to this point? It is the Penitential Act of the Mass that gives us this healthy dose of humility. Through the Penitential Act, we prepare ourselves to celebrate the sacred mysteries of the Mass by acknowledging our failures and asking the Lord for pardon and strength.

As a result of the opening procession, we find ourselves face-to-face with God, who showers us with overwhelming love and mercy. And so, we can't help but become more aware of our own imperfections. We enter into the Penitential Act, in which we present these imperfections to God and ask him to shower us with mercy.

Contrition, sorrow, forgiveness—these are powerful qualities with far-reaching consequences when they converge. And so it should come as no surprise that expressing sorrow for our sinfulness—both personal and communal— and humbly asking God for forgiveness are the first things we do at Mass immediately after gathering. We do this during the part of the Mass called the Penitential Act. Little by little, the Mass challenges us to acknowledge that we are not the center of the universe. As these Introductory Rites continue to gather us into community, the Penitential Act reminds us that this is a community of sinners, all in need of a little humility. The Penitential Act reminds us that there is a need—indeed, an ongoing need—to seek forgiveness for our sins. Certainly there is a need at the beginning of every liturgy to prepare ourselves for the awesome mystery of Christ's death and resurrection, which we are about to celebrate, and for the body and blood of Christ, of which we are about to partake. This emphasis on sin is a stark reminder of the world to which we will return and in which we will live. Our world is filled with the grace of God, but it is also a sinful world, sadly made more sinful by our own deeds and omissions. So before we do anything else in the liturgy, it is crucial that we admit the sinfulness in which we have willingly participated and humbly ask for forgiveness. It is similar to the experience described in the story at the start of this chapter: standing before the coach quietly, not making excuses, just being honest. The fact that we will return to this theme numerous times throughout the liturgy reinforces the importance of the Penitential Act, which challenges us to resist the sinfulness we will encounter when we leave the church after Mass. The sacred liturgy's message to us is that contrition and forgiveness are not a one-moment-in-history event but an ongoing process made necessary by our sinful condition.

The Penitential Act has three formats, not including the rite for the blessing and sprinkling of water (this rite reminds us of the forgiveness of sins we received in baptism).

The first form is the simple "I confess" prayer, also known as the *Confiteor* (from the Latin for "I confess"). It is the most personal of the forms, worded in the first-person singular. As we pray, "through my fault, through my fault, through my most grievous fault," we symbolically strike our breast three times, recalling the humble tax collector who went up to the Temple to pray and beat his breast saying, "God, be merciful to me, a sinner!" (Luke 18:13)

> I confess to almighty God
> and to you, my brothers and sisters,

that I have greatly sinned,
in my thoughts and in my words,
in what I have done and in what I have failed to do,
through my fault, through my fault,
through my most grievous fault;
therefore I ask blessed Mary ever-Virgin,
all the Angels and Saints,
and you, my brothers and sisters,
to pray for me to the Lord our God.

The second form, in some ways the simplest penitential prayer, is a quiet admission of our sinfulness, accompanied with a request for mercy and love. It is a simple prayer reminiscent of the words spoken by the tax collector in the parable of the Pharisee and the tax collector (see Luke 18:9–14), who stood at the back of the temple, lowered his head, beat his breast, and humbly asked forgiveness:

Priest: Have mercy on us, O Lord.
People: For we have sinned against you.

Priest: Show us, O Lord, your mercy.
People: And grant us your salvation.

The third form contains invocations to which the assembly responds by asking for mercy:

Priest: You were sent to heal the contrite of heart:
    Lord, have mercy.
People: Lord, have mercy.

Priest: You came to call sinners:
　　　Christ, have mercy.
People: Christ, have mercy.

Priest: You are seated at the right hand of the
　　　Father to intercede for us:
　　　Lord, have mercy.
People: Lord, have mercy.

All three forms end with the priest praying an absolution, a "washing away," or forgiveness, of our sins:

Priest: May almighty God have mercy on us,
　　　forgive us our sins,
　　　and bring us to everlasting life.
People: Amen.

Finally, if we have not already used the invocations "Lord, have mercy . . . Christ, have mercy . . . Lord, have mercy" in one of the forms of the Penitential Act, we do so in the vernacular or in Greek:

Priest: Lord, have mercy.　　Kyrie, eleison.
People: Lord, have mercy.　　Kyrie, eleison.

Priest: Christ, have mercy.　　Christe, eleison.
People: Christ, have mercy.　　Christe, eleison.

Priest: Lord, have mercy.　　Kyrie, eleison.
People: Lord, have mercy.　　Kyrie, eleison.

Through the Penitential Act, it becomes very clear that before we can move forward in this liturgy, we must sincerely express sorrow for the sins we have carried with us to the altar of God. In fact, the theme of contrition and forgiveness is so important that it recurs during the Mass many times. It reappears seasonally in the Collect Prayer that concludes the Introductory Rites, especially during Lent. Certainly it is the focus of many of the readings proclaimed in sacred Scripture throughout the year and so becomes the cornerstone of many of the homilies we hear. We offer petitions asking for forgiveness. Occasionally, we pray one of the Eucharistic Prayers of Reconciliation, which emphasize the forgiving and healing nature of the liturgy and make these themes central by incorporating them into the very heart of the Mass. We ask for forgiveness by name when we pray the words of the Lord's Prayer. We repeat our request for God's loving mercy in the Lamb of God as we admit our sinfulness just prior to receiving the body and blood of Christ. This is followed by our acknowledgment of Jesus' ability to take away the world's sin, and of our own sinfulness and unworthiness to receive the Eucharist. The liturgy itself can be perceived as a penitential act.

This emphasis on penitence in the celebration of the Eucharist is better understood if we step away from the liturgy and briefly look at its connection to another sacrament of initiation. Because baptism initiates our journey of faith as new Christians and is the very first ritual cleansing of sin, we are offered a reminder of it in the Penitential Act. The priest has the option of doing a rite for the blessing and sprinkling of water. Because this rite echoes and reminds us of the death to sin and new life in Christ we find in the waters of baptism, the rite for the blessing and sprinkling of water, when prayed, replaces the Penitential Act. Often this sprinkling rite is celebrated during the Easter season using the holy water blessed on Holy Saturday night and used in the baptisms that are performed during the Easter Vigil.

In many churches, the baptismal font is located so that the faithful can dip fingers in the holy water and make the sign of the cross upon entering the church and on the way out after the liturgy. These moments help us remember our baptism; they serve as signs of contrition for our sins and, ultimately, as signs of the blessing we take with us when the Mass is ended.

> Hollywood and popular fiction can come up with some really great lines. They can also come up with some unbelievably stupid ones. For me, one of the stupidest lines ever included in a film is the famous line from *Love Story* in which Ali MacGraw says to Ryan O'Neal, "Love means never having to say you're sorry." I don't know of any relationship that has survived without including the magic words *I'm sorry.* I know that in my marriage, I have learned quite the opposite—namely, that love means saying that you're sorry over and over and over again. Not in the sense of groveling, but simply in the sense of letting the other person know that you know what they've suspected all along: that you are not entirely perfect! (JSP)

Like every other moment in the liturgy, there is a dynamic at work in the Penitential Act pointing to the moment when we will find ourselves back on the steps of the church, returning to the routine of our lives. We are humbled by our admission of sinfulness, strengthened by the Eucharist, and challenged to face the very temptations to which we had previously succumbed, now knowing that they cannot defeat us unless we choose to let them. This enables us to be filled with hope and newly aware of grace. Far from being humiliated by our failures, paralyzed by guilt, or haunted with a sense of helplessness, we are changed and energized. We leave church knowing that sinfulness has lost its grip on us.

In the Penitential Act, we come to recognize that God's love and mercy are so much greater than our weaknesses. Because of this, we don't dwell on our sins during the Penitential Act, but rather, we acknowledge our sins and then turn our attention to the only things that can overcome them—God's infinite mercy and love. Humility is not the act of beating ourselves up but of acknowledging that we are in the presence of someone greater than ourselves. To be humble is to embrace vulnerability. Just think of how humbling it is to be visited by people when we're in the hospital, wearing one of those flimsy gowns that never quite cover our derriere, and with no opportunity to "put on our face." Strange, isn't it, that this is precisely when the church deems it crucial and necessary to visit people? Why? Because humility leads to vulnerability, and it is only when we are vulnerable that grace becomes possible. In the same way, when we come face-to-face with God's overwhelming mercy, we are humbled. And this humility is key to our ability to truly celebrate the Eucharist, because when we are vulnerable, we become open to grace. And so in the Penitential Act, we humble ourselves as we pray, "I confess to almighty God. . . ." We are basically turning to one another, removing all pretenses, and saying, "Hi, I'm a sinner. Oh, you are too? Nice to meet you."

In our daily lives, living the Mass means to awaken each day to this realization, to honestly accept our sinfulness, ask forgiveness for it, and open ourselves up to God's mercy so that we in turn can share that mercy with others. To live the Mass is to acknowledge our brokenness but to give praise and glory for the salvation we find in Christ Jesus. In appreciation of this incredible mercy, we are compelled to give glory to God, which is precisely what we do next at Mass. What a great idea! Instead of wallowing in our sins, we joyfully offer praise for God's gift of mercy by singing the Gloria. With the exception of Lent and Advent, the liturgies of Sundays and special feast days invite us to echo the hymn of the Christmas angels who sang of God's glory revealed to a waiting world. We joyfully proclaim that God has been born among us as one who is like us, for one specific reason—to carry on his shoulders the burdens of the sins we have just confessed and to redeem us in the process. Indeed, God never fails to have the mercy on us that we have just so humbly prayed to receive.

> Glory to God in the highest,
> and on earth peace to people of good will.
>
> We praise you,
> we bless you,
> we adore you,
> we glorify you,
> we give you thanks for your great glory,

Lord God, heavenly King,
O God, almighty Father,

Lord Jesus Christ, Only Begotten Son,
Lord God, Lamb of God, Son of the Father,
you take away the sins of the world,
    have mercy on us;
you take away the sins of the world,
    receive our prayer.
you are seated at the right hand of the Father,
    have mercy on us.

For you alone are the Holy One,
you alone are the Lord,
you alone are the Most High,
Jesus Christ,
with the Holy Spirit,
in the glory of God the Father.
Amen.

To receive glory is to be in the spotlight, to be the center of attention. To sing the Gloria is to shift the spotlight off ourselves and onto God, where it belongs. We follow the example of Mary who, upon finding out how God had chosen her for a special role, turned the spotlight, not on herself, but on God. She could have said, "Hey, look at me! I'm the one God chose!" Instead she sang a song of praise, her Magnificat: "My soul magnifies the Lord, and my spirit rejoices in God my savior." In the Gloria, we do likewise: we proclaim that "you alone are the Holy One. You alone are the Lord. You alone are the Most High, Jesus Christ!"

In daily life, living the Mass calls us to bring glory not to ourselves but to God. Each of us is called to live according to that great Jesuit motto *Ad Majorem Dei Gloriam*—"for the greater glory of God." To live the Mass is to live in such a way that we shine the spotlight on God's goodness, showing his love and mercy to those we meet. So even as we leave the Penitential Act with this healthy dose of humility, anticipating God's presence in the sacred Scriptures we are about to hear, we bask in this opportunity to ask God for mercy in the *Gloria*. When we encounter God's glory, all we can do is ask forgiveness for our sins. This clears the way for us to fully enter into the joy of God's presence. Following a brief prayer called the Collect, in which the priest "collects" the individual prayers of the assembly and presents them to God in a unified voice, we now officially enter into the Liturgy of the Word.

The Other Six Days of the Week

With regard to daily life, the Penitential Act invites and challenges us to

- live with a healthy sense of humility;

- forgive others as God forgives us;

- refrain from passing judgment on others, for we are no better or worse than our sisters and brothers;

- find God's mercy and unconditional love as they are shared with us in so many grace-filled moments;

- start to do better than we have done before;

- never give up, because we can always start again with forgiveness;

- be honest about ourselves to ourselves and to others;

- live in the joy of God's glorious love for us.

■ ■ ■

My little children, I am writing these things to you so that you may not sin. But if anyone does sin, we have an advocate with the Father, Jesus Christ the righteous; and he is the atoning sacrifice for our sins, and not for ours only but also for the sins of the whole world.

1 John 2:1–2

4

Ordinary Lives in an Extraordinary Context

The Scripture Readings

When I have a day to myself during the summer, I enjoy heading out to the forest preserve, renting a rowboat, and paddling out to the middle of the lake, where I drop anchor and just sit and relax. I have a habit, however, of getting into the boat facing the wrong way. Accustomed to getting into a car facing the front of the car, I tend to climb into the boat facing the front (the narrow part) of the boat. The rental employee has to remind me to turn around. I keep forgetting that when you row a boat, you face the back of the boat, not the front. Basically, we row backward. Our eyes are on our "past," our point of origin. Every so often, we glance over our shoulder to take a peek at "the future," where we are heading. There's a lesson in that. In the spiritual life, we are moving forward, but we do so with our eyes on the past and only an occasional glimpse to the future. We know the past, but we don't know the future. As we look back, we can more easily recognize God's presence and movement

in the events we've already experienced. Knowing that
God has touched our lives in the past, we can be more
confident about the present and more hopeful about
the future. (JSP)

We leave the Mass with confidence in the present and
hope for the future because of the evidence we find of God's
saving action in the past. How is this accomplished? Through
the Scripture readings of the Liturgy of the Word, we are
reminded of God's great deeds, prompting us to exclaim,
"Thanks be to God!" and "Praise to you, Lord Jesus Christ!"
The Scripture readings illustrate that God is most easily recognized through the rearview mirror (and is closer than he
appears!). The Scripture readings are powerful reminders
that God has taken the initiative and has accomplished many
marvelous deeds throughout salvation history. The Liturgy
of the Word teaches us that it is impossible for us to be spiritually proactive. To be proactive is to be the one who initiates. Scripture tells us the story of how God has already acted
in the past, taking the initiative to reconcile us to himself.
Now it's up to us to respond.

Living the Mass means to remember each and every day
what God has done for us, to recall his great deeds, and to
tell others about them. To live the Mass means to look back
over our own lives and to recognize God's fingerprints in
our comings and goings and to invite others to learn how to
see as well. The stories from Scripture that are proclaimed
to us during the Liturgy of the Word provide an amazing
context for us in which to place our lives. As we hear stories
about how God has acted in extraordinary ways in the lives

of his people, we come to recognize that he has been acting in extraordinary ways in our lives, too. The readings are not simply recitations of events from long ago, but proclamations of a living Word. In response, we celebrate *Eucharist*, a word that comes from the Greek *eucharistia*, meaning "to give thanks," because we have something in our past and in the present for which we are clearly thankful. We are able to pray to the Father about the present and the future with confidence and hope because the evidence of God's faithfulness in the past is overwhelming. We say "Thanks be to God" after the first two readings and "Praise to you, Lord Jesus Christ" after the Gospel because we recognize the presence of God with us now through the Scripture stories. We proclaim "Alleluia!" (except for the season of Lent) before hearing the Gospel, because we know that what we are about to hear is good news. We trace a cross with our thumb on our forehead, lips, and chest as we silently pray, "May God's word be in my mind, on my lips, and in my heart," as a sign of our desire to carry this good news within us and then to share it with others. Having heard the Scripture stories about how God saves, we have no hesitation to proclaim Jesus (whose name means "God saves") to the world. For those who ask us why they should trust in the Lord, we respond with evidence from our past—stories from Scripture that illustrate "our" distant past and stories from our present lives that illustrate how God continues to act in our ongoing history.

Throughout Scripture, God is revealed, not only directly, but also through the testimony of others. By entering into the Scripture stories, we become witnesses, or in Greek, *martyrs*. Certainly the martyrs are those Christians who gave witness to the risen Christ by giving up their own lives. However, the early

Christians understood the word *martyr* to refer to all those who, through their words and deeds, lived as trusted witnesses to the presence of the risen Christ. We have no empirical proof of the tenets of our faith. However, we carry overwhelming and convincing evidence that God saves. We are compelled to present ourselves to the world as martyrs—witnesses of God's salvation through Jesus Christ. Our "testimony" is our way of life. As St. Francis of Assisi is said to have taught, "We proclaim the Good News . . . and sometimes we even use words."

The stories from Scripture proclaimed during the Liturgy of the Word are arranged in a book called the Lectionary, enabling us to hear about God's saving deeds repeatedly throughout the seasons of our lives. Like people rowing boats, we move farther and farther from shore but strive to never lose sight of where we have been so that we can return safely. Our faith journey is addressed through a yearly liturgical calendar and a three-year cycle of Sunday Scripture readings.

What do you do when you visit the Grand Canyon? My wife and kids and I did what everybody does—we oohed and aahed at the first glance of this marvel. We stood at the first lookout point and admired the vast majesty, aware that we could scarcely take in all of it at once. Then we began strolling the path along the rim, glancing over our shoulders as we walked, still trying to comprehend this vast work of art. Farther down the path, we came to another lookout point, where we stopped to take some pictures and do some more oohing and aahing. We were looking at the same reality as

> we were from our first lookout point but from a differ-
> ent perspective. From this new perspective, different
> features of the canyon took on more prominence. In a
> similar way, this is what we do throughout the liturgi-
> cal year. Each season or feast is another "lookout point"
> at which we pause to reflect on the paschal mystery of
> Jesus from a unique perspective. (JSP)

We encounter the reality of Christ in much the same way that
we look at something as immense and deep as the Grand
Canyon. The paschal mystery of Christ—his life, suffering,
death, and resurrection—is so expansive and wondrous that
we "scarce can take it in" (from the traditional Christian
hymn "How Great Thou Art"), and so we encounter it repeatedly through the liturgical calendar and cycle of readings.
We "gaze upon" the paschal mystery from various vantage
points, sometimes pausing to more intensely take in specific angles (Advent, Christmas, Lent, Easter), while at other
times strolling along the path with our gazes fixed on the
entire reality (Ordinary Time).

Our liturgical year—a symbolic ordering of our faith
journey—begins with Advent (the four Sundays prior to
Christmas). The Scripture readings of Advent provide an
opportunity to focus on *hope*. We connect our longings to
the longings the people of Israel had for the coming of the
Messiah. We hear the words of the prophets and of John
the Baptist announcing the coming of the Messiah, and we
come away knowing that we do not hope in vain: Our past
teaches us to always, always have hope in the future. The
Advent Scripture readings teach us that to be a follower

of Jesus is to lead a life of joyful and hope-filled anticipation—not just for the celebration of Christmas but for the entire year.

The Scripture readings of Christmas invite us to reflect on the presence of Jesus through his Incarnation—the act of God becoming human. We hear the stories of Jesus' birth and his epiphany—the revealing of God's human face to the entire world. We celebrate our human condition because it is infused with the divine presence of Jesus. We come away knowing that wherever we go and whatever we do, Jesus, our Emmanuel (meaning "God is with us"), is by our side. We don't need to be afraid, because we are not alone. We don't need to see others as strangers, because God's face is revealed in the human condition. Through the Incarnation, God made it possible for us to see the face of Jesus in the faces of ordinary people.

The Lenten season (the forty days of preparation for Easter) features Scripture readings that call us to reflect on what it means and what it takes to follow Jesus as a disciple. We hear stories of how Jesus overcame temptation, as we consider the ways in which we are tempted. We hear stories that reveal Jesus' ability to save and protect us, and we also hear stories that illustrate what kind of commitment is required of us as followers of Jesus. We ponder more closely the mystery of the cross and reflect on how our suffering can be redemptive. We come away with our priorities rearranged and our focus sharpened.

The profound Scripture readings of Holy Week, especially of the Easter Triduum (Holy Thursday, Good Friday, and Holy Saturday), take us right to the heart of our faith—"We proclaim your Death, O Lord, and profess your

Resurrection until you come again." We hear the sobering stories of denial and betrayal by Jesus' closest friends, and we recognize our own lack of courage and commitment. We hear stories of Jesus' surrender to his Father's will and of the violently cruel treatment he received for remaining faithful to that commitment. We hear stories of suffering and death, and come face-to-face with the paradox of faith—that in order to live, we must die. We come away knowing that even in our darkest moments we can turn to Jesus because he, too, has experienced the deepest darkness.

The joyful Scripture readings of the fifty days of Easter (beginning with the Sunday after the first full moon of spring) provide an opportunity to celebrate the new life that comes about through the transformation of death. We hear stories of the risen Jesus appearing to his disciples, and we come away knowing that he walks among us today. We are confident that if God can overcome death, he can overcome anything. During the Easter season, we celebrate our belief that the Spirit of the risen Lord is right here, in the community of faith, giving us both the desire and the ability to share the Good News.

The Scripture readings of Ordinary Time (between Christmas and Lent, and again between Pentecost and Advent) invite us to explore the vast expanse of the paschal mystery of Christ in the same way that we take in the vastness of the Grand Canyon as we stroll between lookout points. The Scripture readings teach us that there is nothing ordinary about Ordinary Time. Aware of God's presence and continuing love, the church does not let a day go by without counting it as belonging to God. Because we count our Sundays in this way, we call them Ordinary, as in the word *ordinal,* meaning "numbered." Because we encounter, day by day and Sunday after Sunday, the deeds of the Lord proclaimed in Scripture, we are reminded regularly that this moment and every moment belong to God.

Most of us have suffered through a variety of lectors, from the overly dramatic ones who call attention to themselves to the other extreme—the totally unprepared ones who stumble and fumble their way painfully through the word of God. Fortunately, most lectors fall somewhere between these extremes. However, every once in a while, we witness a very special moment when God's word has been so seared into the heart of the one reading it that he or she truly proclaims it, and the experience of the reading is illuminated by grace. All of us in the congregation come face-to-face, heart-to-heart, with God's presence, which is at once loving and mysterious. Karen's reading on Good Friday of Isaiah's description of the suffering servant was one of those unforgettable moments. When she had completed the reading, a reverent hush enveloped the assembly. Karen solemnly said, "The word of the Lord." The congregation, still transfixed by the proclamation, remained silent—collectively at a loss for words. After a moment, and with great humility, Karen said the words again, softly: "The word of the Lord." This time, the assembly found its tongue and responded with a prayerful, "Thanks be to God." As Karen walked back to her seat, everyone stood—a spontaneous tribute, not to her but to the living word she had just proclaimed. (DJG)

The word of God is alive, and it is to be proclaimed with authority. In the early church, someone who taught with authority was perceived as a person who enabled others to act upon what they learned. Jesus taught with authority because his words made it possible for people to act upon God's call to holiness. When we receive the word of God, we become witnesses who can speak with authority—not bullies who force others to act the way we think they should, but people who, through our words and actions, propose a viable way to live as disciples of Jesus.

When we live each day with an awareness that our lives find meaning when connected to the word of God, we recognize that our lives take place in the context of a vast, ongoing story. The next part of the Liturgy of the Word, the homily, helps us reinterpret our seemingly ordinary lives within this extraordinary context.

The Other Six Days of the Week

With regard to daily life, the Scripture readings of the Liturgy of the Word invite and challenge us to

- live in confidence, knowing that God's great deeds of the past are continuing in the present and will continue in the future;

- speak and act as witnesses to God's saving power;

- place our lives within a context of God's plan of salvation;

- live with an awareness that all time belongs to God and that no single moment is ordinary;

- open ourselves to the transformation that comes from placing God at the center of our lives;

- recognize that we live our lives in response to God, who has already actively reached out to us;

- live with an appreciation for the past, acceptance of the present, and hope for the future;

- look more closely for evidence of God's loving presence in daily life;

- speak God's word with authority, enabling others to act upon it;

- keep a Bible close at hand and read from it regularly.

■ ■ ■

We also constantly give thanks to God for this, that when you received the word of God that you heard from us, you accepted it not as a human word but as what it really is, God's word, which is also at work in you believers.

1 Thessalonians 2:13

5

Making Sense out of Life

The Homily

The newly ordained associate pastor preached his first homily at the Saturday evening Mass. He used every tool and technique he had learned in the seminary— every single one. This, unfortunately, made for a thirty-five-minute homily that few were able to comprehend. The smile melted from his face as he saw me waiting on the church steps gazing at my watch. When he looked at his own, he jumped back in horror. He couldn't believe how long Mass had taken. In a soft voice he asked me what had happened. I simply told him that he would be giving homilies for the next fifty years of his life and that there was no need to say everything in the first one! (DJG)

It is through the homily—the reflection offered by the priest or deacon following the Gospel—that we reinterpret our lives in light of the Scripture readings. The homily nurtures our

Christian lives, bringing together some aspect of the Scripture readings with the day-to-day needs of God's people.

A homily need not wow us or entertain us in order to be effective. In fact, a homily should not be judged by its entertainment value. A successful homily is measured in terms of its real impact on people when they leave church and return to their homes or schools, neighborhoods, or workplaces. Because the people of God have a profound responsibility to carry out the mission of Jesus Christ when they leave the church, they have a right to excellent homilies that will assist them.

The homily is one of the most dramatic moments of the Mass because the congregation does not know how it will unfold. The homily is one of the few times in the Mass when the words and gestures have not been predetermined. The combination of high expectations of the hearers and the human limitations of the homilist simply add to the drama: What can a mere mortal say about God's immortal word? When you stop to think about it, what could be harder for a homilist to do than to follow God's own word—the readings from sacred Scripture with all their richness—with his own words? The word of God spans centuries, with stories handed down from generation to generation, as well as songs, visions, prophecies, the words and deeds of Jesus the Messiah, and the letters of the apostles. Following the proclamation of these stories, the congregation sits down and waits to hear the homilist reflect on what has just been shared in Scripture. The people of God sit silently, bearing the invisible baggage of their unique experiences, emotions, desires, hopes, and dreams. So, just what can and should we expect from a homily? That can be answered in one word: *transformation.*

How can ten or eight, or even seven minutes transform our lives? If we look at how the homily's role in the Mass has evolved over the history of the church, we can better understand its role today. The homily has had an interesting history over the centuries since Jesus first broke bread with his disciples in the upper room on the night before he died. Many of the fathers of the early church wrote sermons for specific liturgical celebrations that are masterful treatises on various aspects of the Catholic faith. Many of these sermons, in manuscript form, are as long as a book and represent some of the most advanced philosophical, theological, and pastoral thinking of their time. At other times, homilies were short or altogether absent from the Mass. The reality of unevenly educated clergy speaking to typically uneducated congregations in Gothic churches before the invention of amplification made it easy for this aspect of the liturgy to be downplayed. Throughout the centuries, however, the church has been graced with many masterful preachers whose words needed to be heard at specific intervals in history. A single homily could launch a crusade, bring down a king, or raise enough funds to keep the Papal States afloat. Or, one homily could bring countless numbers to repentance, to lay down their arms, to stop rioting, and most important, to change their hearts. At the right time and place, and coming from the right speaker, a homily can be powerful beyond its words.

In the sixteenth century, the Reformation, with its emphasis on Scripture, resulted in the development of Protestant preachers who emphasized preaching the word of God. At the same time, the Catholic Church, suspicious of too much emphasis on the word of God, focused much more attention on the sacramental life: sign, symbol, and ritual. From the time of the Council of Trent until the Second Vatican Council in the 1960s, the homily gradually lost its importance in the Catholic Mass. Some of us may be old enough to remember homily-free Masses during the summer months because of the excessive heat. However, since the reforms of the Second Vatican Council and the bishops' call to "fully conscious and active participation" in the Mass, the homily's importance has been reaffirmed. For most Catholics today, it is difficult to picture Mass without a homily.

The church uses the word *homily* to describe the part of the Mass that was once (and sometimes still is) referred to as the "sermon." What's the difference? While they are similar, a sermon tends to be a series of doctrinal explanations or moral exhortations on various themes or topics, while a homily is an interpretation of life in light of the liturgy's Scripture readings. A sermon is preached *at* a congregation and tends to give answers, while a homily, in many ways, challenges us to actively ask ourselves the right questions. Whereas a sermon provides an answer key for living, a homily gives us an assignment, namely, the task of applying the word of God to our unique life situations. A good homily does not preach *about* Jesus—it preaches Jesus. A homilist does not talk about God but leads the people of God into an encounter with the living God who is present in the liturgy.

The homily, based on the liturgy and Scriptures that have been proclaimed, strives to help us take that word of God with us when we leave the church. In order to accomplish this, a good homily, according to author Daniel E. Harris in *We Speak the Word of the Lord,* must

- proclaim Scripture;

- witness the faith;

- be imaginative;

- be hopeful;

- be in touch with people's lives;

- be engaging;

- have one central idea;

- be clear and simple.

When done well, the homily enters our lives. Our stories become the conduit for the larger story of salvation history that has been partly opened up for us in the homily. The work of the homily is not accomplished in a vacuum. The homilist is not a lecturer delivering talks on a pre-chosen theme with no regard for current events, the experiences of those gathered, or the time of year (liturgical year, that is). On the contrary, a homily speaks directly to our human experiences relating to the word of God. Only then can a homilist hope to inspire transformation in the listeners.

Like my dad, my uncle Joe was a pharmacist, and I had the chance to work alongside him as a pharmacy technician for many years at his store. Once, a customer was giving my uncle a really hard time, accusing him of all sorts of dishonest practices. I waited for my uncle to explode at him with a sharp and swift comeback that would put the customer in his place. When the customer finally finished his tirade, my uncle took a deep breath and calmly said, "I'm sorry you feel that way." I'm certain there were many more things my uncle wanted to say, but he showed amazing self-control and brought a quick end to what could have been an even worse situation. I learned from my uncle Joe how to look at difficult situations in a new way, and whenever I found myself in a similar situation, I tried to see with uncle Joe's eyes. On that particular day (and many others besides), uncle Joe was a living homily, inviting me through his actions to see through another set of eyes, eyes that see as Jesus sees. (JSP)

The Gospels compel us to look at life differently. That's what a good homily attempts to do. Homilies are less about information and more about transformation. A good homily makes it possible for us to act on our beliefs. The Scriptures tell us that Jesus taught with authority: "They were astounded at his teaching, because he spoke with authority" (Luke 4:32). Jesus made it possible for people to act upon God's law. A good homily does the same.

When listening to a homily, we don't wait to be entertained but to be changed. Even if a homily is done poorly, we still have the ability to reflect personally on how the Gospel is calling us to change today and in the days ahead. A good homilist, however, is capable of proposing a new and viable way of looking at reality. In many ways, a good homily does the opposite of the familiar "good news/bad news" jokes that present the good news first only to negate it with the bad. A good homily first presents the "bad news"—those things in

life that seem to be obstacles to our attempts to find fulfillment—and then introduces the good news of Jesus Christ
in a way we can internalize and carry with us. We, in turn,
become living homilies as we leave the church: messages of
good news that overcome the bad news.

Church history is full of living homilies: Thomas à
Kempis, St. Francis of Assisi, Blessed Teresa of Calcutta, and
many others who walked the streets smiling, sharing alms,
embracing the lonely, and serving others, making it possible for people to consider an alternate vision of reality. No
doubt, there are people in your life who have been, and continue to be, living homilies for you. In the same way, when we
leave Mass and go forth into the world, we are called to be
living homilies, doing the work of evangelization by inviting
others to consider the good news of Jesus Christ as a viable
alternative to their present way of life. We don't have to be
great orators to be living homilies. We don't have to stand on
street corners or gather people around water coolers in order
to "preach" the good news of Jesus. If our lives offer viable
alternatives to despair, hatred, oppression, injustice, bigotry,
prejudice, greed, dishonesty, violence, and other evils, we are
indeed offering ourselves to others as living homilies.

The real measure of a homily's effectiveness is not
whether it makes us feel good but whether it moves us to act
when we leave church and return to our homes or schools,
neighborhoods or workplaces. Like the disciples on the road
to Emmaus who asked, "Were not our hearts burning within
us while he was talking to us on the road?" (Luke 24:32), we
are tantalized by words in a homily that offer us a new direction—words that propose hope and new life as an alternative
to despair and death.

With our communities so often diverse in age, background, and so much more, the only way for a homily to speak to all people is for it to center on the universal truths of the Scriptures and the history and tradition of the church. These truths are proclaimed boldly and without fear following the homily when we make our profession of faith. Our recitation of the Nicene Creed is our proclamation of the Christian way of seeing reality—a transformed way of seeing made possible by God's living word proclaimed in the Scripture readings and the homily.

The Other Six Days of the Week

With regard to daily life, the homily of the Mass invites and challenges us to

- be transformed and look at our world differently;

- take our faith with us wherever we go when we leave the church;

- become living homilies by living out what we believe in our actions;

- reflect on God's presence and what that means in our lives;

- integrate our beliefs with our actions rather than separate and isolate them;

- push ourselves to be better people of faith;

- invite others to consider the good news of Jesus as a viable alternative to their present way of life.

■ ■ ■

The sermon, moreover, should draw its content mainly from scriptural and liturgical sources, and its character should be that of a proclamation of God's wonderful works in the history of salvation, the mystery of Christ, ever made present and active within us, especially in the celebration of the liturgy.

Constitution on the Sacred Liturgy
Second Vatican Council

6

In God We Trust

The Profession of Faith

Caveat emptor. You don't have to know Church Latin to recognize those two words: "Buyer beware." When investing our money in a product or service, we need to know that we can trust the seller. When my wife and I were newly married and in search of our first new car, we didn't know a thing about the intricacies of car buying. We went into the dealer and told him that both of our old cars were dying and that we were desperate for a new car. The seemingly nice old salesman we placed our trust in was more than happy to take advantage of us. We ended up with a deal that probably pushed up his retirement date by a few months and set ours back a few years! This experience, however, has not prevented me from stepping into auto showrooms. I've become much better at forcing the seller to establish trust so that we can bargain in good faith. When trust is betrayed, we can either decide never to trust again, or we can enter into new relationships—whether personal or professional—with our eyes opened, seeking the knowledge upon which a trusting relationship can be formed. (JSP)

When we leave church, we are meant to go with a sense of conviction, trusting in the God who has placed his trust in us by accepting us as disciples of his Son, Jesus. We go with a vocabulary that enables us to express our limited understanding of a God who transcends human understanding. We go with some memory of God's face, which has been revealed to us. How do we come to this point? It is through our profession of faith, the creed, that we express our faith in—and allow our faith to be shaped by—God, who is Father, Son, and Holy Spirit.

"Trust me." Those two words can be very frightening. When someone asks us to trust him or her, that person is inviting us into a relationship. To place our trust in someone is to let him or her lead the way as we follow. To trust in someone is to surrender our own will to theirs. At times, we have no choice but to trust in someone who claims to be an expert at something we know nothing about, whether it be brain surgery or auto mechanics. From the time we are infants, we learn to trust in others. If we trust that someone is good and friendly, we are attracted to them. If we trust that an object or toy will not harm us, we approach it.

When we say, "I believe in one God," we are saying that we trust God. To pray the words of the creed at Mass is to proclaim a relationship. All too often we think of the creed as a list of doctrinal statements to which we have sworn intellectual assent and adherence. Perhaps if we inserted the word *trust* wherever the word *believe* appears, we would have a different understanding of what it means to profess our faith.

> I believe [trust] in one God,
> the Father almighty,
> maker of heaven and earth,
> of all things visible and invisible.

> I believe [trust] in one Lord Jesus Christ,
> the Only Begotten Son of God,
> born of the Father before all ages.
> God from God, Light from Light,
> true God from true God,
> begotten, not made, consubstantial with the Father;
> through him all things were made.
> For us men and for our salvation
> he came down from heaven,
> and by the Holy Spirit was incarnate of the Virgin
>   Mary,
> and became man.

> For our sake he was crucified under Pontius
>   Pilate;
> he suffered death and was buried,
> and rose again on the third day
> in accordance with the Scriptures.
> He ascended into heaven
> and is seated at the right hand of the Father.
> He will come again in glory
> to judge the living and the dead
> and his kingdom will have no end.

I believe [trust] in the Holy Spirit, the Lord, the
    giver of life,
who proceeds from the Father and the Son,
who with the Father and the Son is adored
    and glorified,
who has spoken through the prophets.

I believe [trust] in one, holy, catholic and
    apostolic Church.
I confess one Baptism for the forgiveness
    of sins
and I look forward to the resurrection
    of the dead
and the life of the world to come. Amen.

Why do we trust God? Because God has first placed his trust
in us by offering us his unconditional love. He now invites
us to reciprocate. While none of us can claim a perfect
score at maintaining that trust, God has never let us down.
The Scripture readings and homily have just reminded us
of God's unfailing love and of his saving deeds in the past
and in the present. We move forward into the future armed
with confidence because we believe—we trust—in God.
Living the Mass, then, means to live with a radical trust
each and every day of our lives. It means to live without
fear—to "be not afraid"—and to help others to live without fear by placing their trust in God and in his church.
With such trust, we are able to live our lives without fear.
In the Scriptures, one of the most often repeated lines is

the phrase *Fear not* or variations such as "Do not fear," "Be not afraid," "Do not be afraid," or "Do not be troubled." The fact is, in this life, there is much to fear. Although we have justifiable fears about how dangerous our world can be, we tend to have a much greater fear: We fear that God's love will not be enough for us. We do not trust that God's grace is all we need. And so we search for things to place our trust in, only to be betrayed by their inability to satisfy us. Through it all, God invites us to return to him and to place our trust in him. From the beginning of the Bible to the very end, God reaches out to his people, inviting us to overcome fear and place our trust in him. Here are just a few examples:

- "After these things the word of the LORD came to Abram in a vision, 'Do not be afraid, Abram, I am your shield; your reward shall be very great'" (Genesis 15:1).

- "Then he said, 'I am God, the God of your father; do not be afraid to go down to Egypt, for I will make of you a great nation there'" (Genesis 46:3).

- "Do not fear, for I am with you, / do not be afraid, for I am your God; / I will strengthen you, I will help you, / I will uphold you with my victorious right hand" (Isaiah 41:10).

- "Then Jesus said to them, 'Do not be afraid; go and tell my brothers to go to Galilee; there they will see me'" (Matthew 28:10).

- "But overhearing what they said, Jesus said to the leader of the synagogue, 'Do not fear, only believe'" (Mark 5:36).

- "The angel said to her, 'Do not be afraid, Mary, for you have found favor with God'" (Luke 1:30).

- "But [Jesus] said to them, 'It is I; do not be afraid'" (John 6:20).

- "One night the Lord said to Paul in a vision, 'Do not be afraid, but speak and do not be silent'" (Acts 18:9).

- "When I saw him, I fell at his feet as though dead. But he placed his right hand on me, saying, 'Do not be afraid; I am the first and the last'" (Revelation 1:17).

God's trust in us, demonstrated in his willingness to enter into a covenant with us, has never failed, even though we have not always held up our end of the bargain. Rather than seek vengeance on us, however, God seeks reconciliation—a restoring of trust. Even when his closest followers abandoned him at the time of his crucifixion, Jesus responded, "Peace be with you" (John 20:19). Like us, the apostle Thomas could not believe that something good could come out of such an awful experience. He was unable to trust in the Resurrection until Jesus entered back into relationship with him and told him to believe. Thomas responded with a profession of faith: "My Lord and my God!" (John 20:28).

Despite our sinfulness, Jesus offers us reconciliation (recall the Penitential Act). Like Thomas, we respond to this forgiveness by making our profession of faith. As we profess our faith in the creed, we are setting aside our doubts and fears and affirming a trusting relationship—in the Father, who created us and loves us; in the Son, Jesus, who redeems us through his suffering, death, and resurrection; and in the Holy Spirit, who gives us life and teaches us how to trust. We also affirm our trust in the relationship we have with the church—the people of God and the Body of Christ on earth.

> When I was a teenager, I tried really hard to be bad and failed miserably. Like most teenagers, I was struggling to find my identity. I didn't want to be the Goody Two-shoes I had been in grammar school. I wanted to be cool. So I grew my hair long. I dressed like a rebel. I hung out with the cool crowd and did cool things. Or so I thought. In reality, I ended up doing a lot of things that were just plain stupid. I did things that were not me. Why? Because I didn't know who "me" was. Like most teenagers, I went through a difficult period of awkwardly grasping after some identity or meaning. It wasn't until a few years later, when I began to know what I really believed in and who God was calling me to be, that I began to act accordingly. It's so hard to know how to act when you don't know who you are or what you believe in. (JSP)

It can be so enjoyable to observe teenagers. It can also be very painful. Because of their developing bodies and brains, teenagers struggle to define themselves. Their behavior can often be erratic because of their own confusion over who they are and who they want to be. Many teenagers do not trust themselves enough to act with confidence and poise. Without a clear sense of identity, it is difficult to act in a consistent manner. All of us need a clear sense of identity, and in order to have that, we need to know what we believe in.

The creed is a prayer that expresses our identity. We are baptized into this creed. At infant baptisms, it is up to parents and godparents to accept this identity on behalf of the child, as they respond, "I do" to baptismal promises drawn from the creed. To symbolize our new identity, we were given a baptismal garment. We are what we wear! When an adult is welcomed into the church through the sacraments of initiation, he or she is presented with the creed just days before the sacraments are celebrated. The gift of the creed symbolizes the newly forming identities of those about to be baptized. The message is clear: If you wish to be a disciple of Jesus, place your trust in him; know who it is you believe in and why. Supported by firm belief, we can live our lives in a consistent manner.

To have faith and to live in a consistent manner, however, is not to be confused with having absolute certainty. In the Gospel of John, the apostle Thomas experiences doubt about the resurrection of Jesus (see 20:24–29). Unfortunately, Thomas has gotten a bad rap over the ages for his doubt when, in truth, his reaction illustrates the inseparable connection between doubt and faith. Without doubt, faith can turn into moral arrogance. A Lebanese-American poet, philosopher, and artist, Khalil Gibran (1883–1931) wrote that "doubt is a pain too lonely to know that faith is his twin brother."

Scripture illustrates the connection between doubt and faith in Mark 9:14–29, when Jesus encounters the father of a boy who is possessed by a demon. The father says, "if you are able . . . help us," to which Jesus replies, "If you are able!—All things can be done for the one who believes." The father replies, "I believe, help my unbelief!" And Jesus casts out the demon, having moved a man from doubt to faith. To have faith means to be sure of something and to hope for it at the same time. As we grow in faith, we do not become more certain, but we become better at trusting. This trust in God—Father, Son, and Holy Spirit—guides us through moments of doubt and helps us to live day by day as disciples of Jesus Christ.

When we believe that God is our Father and that he is the Creator of all things visible and invisible, we can live as brothers and sisters who treasure one another and all creation. We can live as people who recognize that we are not the ones in control, but that we depend on God, our Creator, for all things. We can get up and go to work each day knowing that, as children of the Creator of the universe, made in his image, we bear a striking family resemblance. How awesome it is for us to come to believe that we are cocreators, participating in God's ongoing creation.

When we believe that Jesus, the Son of God, became one of us, we can live with respect for our own dignity and the dignity of others, knowing that our God has a human face. When we believe that Jesus suffered, died, and rose from the dead, we can live with confidence, knowing that nothing can separate us from the love of God—not even death. When we believe that Jesus will come again, we can live with hope, knowing that we indeed have a future.

When we believe that the Holy Spirit is the Lord, the giver of life, we can live without fear, knowing that we are not alone but that the spirit of the risen Christ is with us at all times.

When we believe that the church is "one holy, catholic, and apostolic Church," we can live as people who seek unity, who seek to do God's will, who embrace diversity, and who are sent to carry on a mission that has been handed on to us by those who walked with Jesus.

When we believe in everlasting life, we can live with perspective and without anxiety, knowing that God has a plan for us to live with him through eternity.

There's only one way to respond to all the above, and it's the last word of the creed: Amen!

The Other Six Days of the Week

With regard to daily life, the creed invites and challenges us to

- place our trust in God—Father, Son, and Holy Spirit;

- live with confidence, conviction, and courage;

- live without fear, and help to dispel fear from the lives of others;

- embrace our doubts as pathways to believing;

- act according to our beliefs and in a way that is fitting with the title *disciple;*

- know and understand words that can help us to articulate what we believe about our relationship with God and the church;

- respect all of God's creation;

- recognize the face of Jesus in all human beings;

- live with a sense of identity, and act accordingly;

- clothe ourselves in Christ each and every day.

■ ■ ■

This is our faith.

This is the faith of the church.

We are proud to profess it in Christ Jesus our Lord.

The rite of baptism

7

Pray as if Your Life Depended on It

The Prayer of the Faithful

Early in my priesthood, on my way to teach classes at the high school seminary, I would stop at a convent to celebrate early morning daily Mass. When it came time for the Prayer of the Faithful, I would offer the opportunity for all the sisters in attendance to share their prayers. At one convent, their prayers unfolded in the same pattern every day, making me painfully aware of the issues and concerns created by their daily community living. After remembering a deceased contemporary or another sister's anniversary of final vows, one of the sisters would launch the opening salvo with a petition that was clearly directed at another sister in the chapel. You could hear the frustration in her voice as she prayed for an end to gossip or for everyone to carry their load. Then, another sister, feeling rightly or not that she was the one being attacked, would pray in self-defense for an increase in Christian charity among all of those who had professed religious vows. This would embolden another of them to pray out of frustration over the behavior of one of the other sisters. And so it would go until the eldest and clearly the wisest sister in the group, with more than a hint of exasperation and sanctity in her voice, would pray that they all might just get along. Mercifully, that petition, perhaps the most desperate, honest, and blunt, would bring about silence so that I could offer the closing prayer of the Prayer of the Faithful. For better or for worse, the Prayer of the Faithful reveals our true selves as we stand before God—desperately begging for the grace we need to cope with life's daily struggles. (DJG)

The Mass sends us forth more vividly aware that we need to pray as if our lives depend on it—because they do. We leave church with a renewed concern for the needs of others and for the needs of the church and the world. We leave with the knowledge that our lives are not complete and that only faith in God can bring fullness of life. We go out into the world reminded that pain and suffering are a reality of this life, but also bolstered in our confidence that God will provide the grace we need to overcome these obstacles. How do we come to this point? It is through the Prayer of the Faithful— prayers offered on the behalf of others—that we learn to approach God, knowing that we will find what we need, that our prayers will be answered, and that the necessary doors will be opened.

Let's face it, we are a troubled people. Day in and day out, we come face-to-face with problems, challenges, sadness, and even tragedy. The question, as posed in the theme song from the movie *Ghostbusters*, is "Who you gonna call?" When you are in trouble, you call on someone who has proven he or she can help. The Scripture readings have just reminded us of God's great deeds in the lives of his people. As a result, we have just expressed, in the Creed, supreme trust in God. It makes sense, now, to call upon God in the Prayer of the Faithful.

What is prayer, really, and what role should it play, not only in liturgy but in life? First, we can take some cues from the early church. In the Acts of the Apostles, we learn that the first Christians believed fervently in the power of prayer. We are told that "they devoted themselves to the apostles' teaching and fellowship, to the breaking of bread and the prayers" (Acts 2:42). St. Paul wrote to the Thessalonians telling them to "pray without ceasing" (1 Thessalonians 5:17). Praying for the needs of the community and of the world was an integral part of the first Eucharistic meals in the early days of the developing church. As believers gathered around the table, they listened to the stories of Jesus and heard the words that he had spoken during his ministry. They were exhorted to live faithful lives as they listened to the public reading of letters from Paul and the other apostles. They shared in the Eucharistic meal and lifted up the names of those who were ill, those who had been martyred, those suffering from persecution, and those with other needs and concerns.

Somewhere along the way, however, these intercessions, known as the Prayer of the Faithful, lost their place in the Mass. Over the centuries, the role of the congregation during Mass became increasingly passive as the priest assumed more and more of the responsibility to offer the prayers on behalf of those gathered. Fortunately, the changes in the Mass that came about as a result of the Second Vatican Council in the 1960s refocused attention on the "fully conscious, and active participation" (*Constitution on the Sacred Liturgy,* 14) of all the faithful in liturgical celebrations. One of the ways this was accomplished was the reinstatement of the Prayer of the Faithful in the liturgy. Today, the *Catechism of the Catholic Church* tells us that, for a follower of Jesus, prayer is not an option: "Prayer and *Christian life* are *inseparable*" (*Catechism of the Catholic Church,* 2745). In fact, prayer is considered one of the four pillars of the Catholic faith, along with the creed, the sacraments, and the moral life.

The Prayer of the Faithful occurs in the Mass exactly when it should. It follows the homily and the Profession of Faith (the creed). Inspired by God's word, challenged to transform our lives, and trusting in the Father, Son, and Holy Spirit, we approach God with our deepest desires, asking for his transforming grace. The gathering rites and the Liturgy of the Word have served to remind us that God is God and we are not. Realizing that we are dependent on God for everything, we instinctively know that we must pray to him. We could not bat an eye or breathe a sigh if not for the grace of God. Grateful for this amazing grace, we turn to the source of life and offer our prayers.

Recognition of this radical dependence on God is at the heart of what it means to be baptized. For this reason, the catechumens—those preparing for baptism—are dismissed from the liturgy before the Profession of Faith and the Prayer of the Faithful. They leave the assembly to further reflect upon God's word. The timing of this dismissal is not haphazard or accidental. Dismissing those who are preparing for baptism before the Profession of Faith and the Prayers of the Faithful sends a message not only to those being dismissed but also to those remaining behind. It tells us that proclaiming absolute trust in God and approaching him in prayer are not to be taken lightly but involve a radical transformation. Those being dismissed are sent to reflect upon their growing desire to make this radical commitment to the Lord that will lead to their baptism in and communion with Jesus. Those remaining behind are not off the hook. We are keenly aware of our limitations and our radical dependence on God. We know that we cannot do the work of the Gospel on our own. So we must pray. In the Prayer of the Faithful, we share our common needs and concerns. Our response is a communal one that reminds us that we are not alone in our task of bringing the gospel of Jesus to the world. We believe with all our hearts that our God who loves us will hear these prayers.

Unlike many of the other parts of the Mass, the Prayer of the Faithful changes from liturgy to liturgy to some extent. Typically, parishioners on a liturgy-planning team or members of the pastoral staff compose the intercessions. Petitions already composed may be taken from prayer books or liturgy aids, but ideally, the prayers are to reflect the Scripture readings for that liturgy, the liturgical season or feast being celebrated, and the particular needs of the community gathered. Likewise, the prayers are to be general enough to include everyone and particular enough to be relevant to all who have gathered for that liturgy. The communal response prayed out loud is intercessory in nature: "Lord, hear us" or "Lord, hear our prayer" or "Lord, save your people."

"All prayer is a response to God!" said my professor, not thinking that anyone would dare to question his authority. Of course, I thought I was smarter, so without hesitation, I thrust my hand up and said, "Excuse me. I don't agree with your statement that *all* prayer is a response to God. What about prayers of petition? When we offer petitions, we are not responding to God. We are initiating the prayer—we are the ones making first contact, and we are praying that God will respond to us." No sooner had I said this than a smirk came across my professor's face, and I realized that I was about to be carved up into little pieces in front of my fellow classmates, who were patting themselves on the back for keeping their mouths shut. "Why do you think we offer petitions to God in the first place?" he asked. "We ask God to hear our prayers," the professor continued, "because we have seen him intervene in so many extraordinary ways in the past—if not in our lives, then in the lives of others. And it is precisely because we have seen God perform wonderful deeds in the past that we *respond* by approaching him to ask for one thing more!" I can attest that, to this day, I believe without a doubt that all prayer is a response to God! (JSP)

So, what and who do we pray for in the Prayer of the Faithful? In a sense, we pray for everything under the sun. Having heard the proclamation of God's wonderful deeds and of his presence in our midst, we respond by approaching him with every concern imaginable. At the same time, following St. Paul's advice to make sure that our liturgies are orderly (see 1 Corinthians 14:26–40), we arrange our requests in an orderly fashion. In fact, the intentions follow a particular order, suggesting to us who and what we should pray for, not only at this liturgy but also throughout the week. After the priest invites the faithful to pray, the intentions, offered by the deacon, a cantor, a lector, or a member of the assembly, generally follow this pattern:

- "For the needs of the church." As baptized members of the church, we pray for the church's mission and for our church leadership.

- "For public authorities and the salvation of the whole world." Knowing that we are at Mass for the express purpose of being sent forth into the world, we pray for the world, for government leaders, and for various world crises that demand our attention.

- "For those burdened by any kind of difficulty." We especially remember the needs of the poor and vulnerable of society.

- "For the local community." We pray for one another and for the needs of our families, parishes, communities, neighborhoods, towns, and villages. We specifically pray for those who are sick, for those who care for them, for those who have died, and for their loved ones.

- For other intentions. Since many of us come with specific needs that others may not be aware of, we are invited to share them with the assembly out loud or to present them to God in silence.

The priest then concludes the Prayer of the Faithful with a prayer that unites all our prayers to God through Jesus. We are then seated, knowing that we have placed our lives in God's hands; trusting in his mercy, care, and compassion; and preparing to enter into deeper communion with his Son, Jesus, who will go with us as we leave.

Because they are prayers that are ever changing to express the needs of those gathered, the Prayer of the Faithful challenges us in specific ways to live out our baptismal call as we leave the church. The Prayer of the Faithful, which brings a close to the Liturgy of the Word, foreshadows the prayers that we will soon place before the altar as we prepare to offer our gifts to the Lord in the Liturgy of the Eucharist.

The Other Six Days of the Week

With regard to daily life, the Prayer of the Faithful invites and challenges us to

- live with an awareness of our total dependence on God;

- pray out of the awareness that we depend on God completely;

- be aware of God's wonderful deeds, and respond by seeking his continuing grace;

- be ever mindful, compassionate, and responsive to the needs of the world and of our local communities;

- reach out to those who are ill and to those who care for them;

- console the families of those who have died;

- bring all of our needs, concerns, and desires to God;

- actively assume our rightful role in the mission of the Church.

■ ■ ■

To save one's soul without prayer is most difficult, and even (as we have seen) impossible. . . . It is not necessary in order to save our souls to go among the heathen, and give up our life. It is not necessary to retire into the desert, and eat nothing but herbs. What does it cost us to say, My God, help me! Lord, assist me! have mercy on me! Is there anything more easy than this? and this little will suffice to save us, if we will be diligent in doing it.

St. Alphonsus Liguori,
The Great Means of Salvation and of Perfection

8

Stewards of God's Gifts

The Presentation of the Gifts

The usher, a self-proclaimed old-timer, came up to me on the steps of the church even before the final hymn of the Mass was over, animatedly telling me about a woman who had put a five-dollar bill in the collection basket and then proceeded to pull out two singles. This had upset him so much that I feared he was going to have a heart attack right in front of me. In all his years as an usher no one had ever done anything like that. And what was I going to do about it? I thanked him for his concern, told him I would handle it, and sent him over to the hall for post-liturgy hospitality. Maybe a donut would soothe him. Before I could catch my breath, the woman he spoke of appeared, right in my face, sobbing uncontrollably, trying to tell me her story. She was not a parishioner. She was on her way to the nursing home up the street to be with her dying sister. She came first to church for Mass. When she put the five-dollar bill in the collection basket, she immediately realized that was all the cash she was carrying. Realizing she needed bus fare home, she panicked, reached in, and pulled out two one-dollar bills. Observing this, the usher had confronted her, accusing her of being a thief. She was obviously upset, feeling angry, guilty, and confused as well. As I tried to assure her everything was all right, I saw the usher heading toward us with a cup of coffee shaking in his hand. Ah, the joys of pastoring! I don't think this is what taking up the collection during the Presentation of the Gifts is supposed to be about. (DJG)

When we "go in peace," we go with a spirit of generosity, knowing that God's grace is more than enough for us. We go back into the world with a desire to share our time, talent, and treasure with others and with God. We are newly aware that, because we have so richly received God's grace and blessings, we in turn are called upon to give to others. How has the Mass brought us thus far to this point? During the Presentation of the Gifts, we offer bread and wine as symbols of our livelihood. Through our offering, we express our belief that we are simply giving back to God that which belongs to God.

The Introductory Rites and the Liturgy of the Word have made it clear that we are on the receiving end of some pretty wonderful things: grace, forgiveness, reconciliation, salvation, fullness of life, and an intimate relationship with a God who can't stop loving us. Up to this point, we have responded in word. Now, as we enter into the Liturgy of the Eucharist, we respond in action.

The Liturgy of the Eucharist begins with a short transitional rite called the Presentation of the Gifts and the Preparation of the Altar. During this rite, members of the assembly bring forward the gifts of bread and wine that will become for us the body and blood of Jesus. In the early days of the church, when Christians assembled in households to celebrate Eucharist, it was customary for people to bring bread and wine for the sacred meal. As the church grew in size, however, this practice became impractical. Now, bread and wine are acquired ahead of time and placed within the assembly so that representatives can bring them forward to the altar.

At the same time, another very important event is taking place: a collection.

Unfortunately, the collection is often viewed solely as a way for the parish to pay its bills. Too many of us in the assembly do not see this collection as a spiritual act—as an expression of the way we hope to live the other six days of the week. If we have entered into the Introductory Rites and the Liturgy of the Word with the proper openness, we should at this point in the Mass recognize without a doubt that God has been giving, giving, and giving. The Introductory Rites and the Liturgy of the Word have reminded us that without the grace of God, we can do nothing. It is the same message, though more subtle, that we receive on Ash Wednesday. To be reminded that we are dust is not an insult to our dignity. To the contrary, we are reminding ourselves of just how lucky we are to have a God who transforms dust into his own image and gives us a share in his creation. In the same way, the Introductory Rites and the Liturgy of the Word have served us this reminder, preparing us to respond with gratitude for the recognition of giftedness.

If we allow the liturgy to speak to us, we come to the realization that only God's grace brings us true fulfillment. In a dramatic scene from the movie *The Exorcist,* the priests conducting the exorcism shout repeatedly at the possessed girl, "The power of CHRIST compels you!" In a much less dramatic way, the liturgy proclaims the same message to us—it is only the power of Christ that compels us. We come to realize what St. Paul once recognized—namely, that next to God's grace, everything else is so much rubbish (see Philippians 3:8). When we recognize that the power of Christ compels us, we are able to let go of those things—money, power, possessions—that we mistakenly think might bring us happiness. Without the realization that the power of Christ compels us, we can more easily fall prey to other "idols" that compel or "possess" us.

In the Profession of Faith, we proclaim our belief and our trust in God as the Creator of all things visible and invisible. In this creed, we are expressing our belief that everything we have is a gift from God. Our response is to live as caretakers of God's gifts and to use them wisely for the good of all. Another word for caretaker is *steward.* Catholics believe that we are called to live as stewards of God's creation—recognizing that all we are and all we have belong to God. Since we ultimately have no ownership of anything but are entrusted with the care of what belongs to God, we cannot hoard anything for ourselves. Stewardship calls us Catholics to care responsibly for God's gifts and to share generously of our time, talent, and treasure.

Stewardship, then, is not a parish program, nor is it ultimately about money. It is an attitude and a way of life. Stewardship is a lifestyle that enhances our relationship with God and with our brothers and sisters by calling us to center our lives on Jesus rather than on ourselves. (Remember the Introductory Rites and their call to overcome narcissistic attitudes?)

Jesus was the ultimate steward. Remember the story of Jesus in the desert for forty days? Like us, he was tempted to center his life on personal comfort, material possessions, and power. However, he opted to center his life not on his own will but on the will of the Father. Jesus generously gave of himself, sharing with others his gifts of teaching and healing, and moving ultimately to the most unselfish act of all— offering his life for others. As disciples of Jesus, we strive to live as he lives.

As followers of Jesus, we live out the call to be stewards in three areas of our lives: time, talent, and treasure. As we look at these three areas, we will also show how the three traditional vows of men and women who live in religious communities—poverty, chastity, and obedience—are radical expressions of the kind of stewardship that we are all called to live in order to sustain a healthy Christian community.

Giving Our Time

We're familiar with the expression "Time is money." This is another way of saying that time is valuable. It is also another way of saying that time is a gift. None of us can claim ownership of the time that has been given to us on this earth. Nor do we know how much of this gift we have been given. We are asked to use the time that has been granted to us in an unselfish way. You may have heard another expression: "No one in their old age says, 'I wish I had spent more time at the office.'" In other words, when we look back on our lives, we tend to evaluate how well we have used our time and whether we used the time given to us to pay attention to the needs of others.

In the famous book *A Christmas Carol,* by Charles Dickens, Ebenezer Scrooge compliments the ghost of his former business partner, Jacob Marley, for being a good businessman. The ghost of Jacob Marley replies with regret, "Business! . . . Mankind was my business! The common welfare was my business; charity, mercy, forbearance, and benevolence were, all, my business. The dealings of my trade were but a drop of water in the comprehensive ocean of my business!" Ebenezer Scrooge does not simply learn a lesson about how he should be using his money but also about how he should be spending his time.

In the same way, the call to follow Jesus more closely is a call to make the most of the time that has been given to us in service to others. We are called to use our time to serve the needs of others at work, at home, with friends, with our parish community, and with our brothers and sisters around the world. The call to stewardship is also a call to ensure that we are allowing time for rest and recreation of our bodies, minds, and spirits. The story of creation in Genesis tells us that God considered rest to be so important that he designated an entire block of time—the Sabbath Day—for what can be considered recreation.

In Catholic tradition, men and women in religious communities take a vow of obedience. This vow is not about a superior saying, "Jump," and a religious responding, "How high?" It is a vow that deals with accountability—how one spends his or her time. Members of religious communities are not "lone rangers" who can come and go as they please. How they spend their time is influenced by the needs of the community. Each of us, as members of various communities—families, parishes, neighborhoods, workplaces— is called to consider the needs of the community when we make decisions about how to spend our time. As baptized Catholics, we are indeed accountable to one another and are called to use our time wisely, not for selfish needs but for the needs of the community.

Giving Our Talent

When we refer to someone as a "gifted" individual, we are referring to his or her abundance of talent in some area of life. No matter what our level of talent may be, however, we are all gifted. God has gifted each of us with talents that can be used in service to others. These talents can be recognized in our skills, in our interests, and in our personalities. The opportunity to use our talents to serve the needs of others and to bring glory to God is, in and of itself, a gift. We do this through our work, through our family life, and through the service we provide to others in our parish community and beyond.

Jesus illustrated the importance of using our God-given talents in a parable that has come to be known as the parable of the talents (see Matthew 25:14–30). In this story, the word *talent* refers to a coin that was of significant value. In this parable, we learn of a man who, before going on a journey, calls in his servants and entrusts his fortune to them: five talents to one, two talents to the second, and one talent to the third. Two of the servants quickly invest their talents and double their amounts, while the servant with one talent buries it out of fear. Upon his return, the master rewards the servants who invested their talents and berates the servant who hid his talent out of fear. Jesus teaches us that our talents—our gifts—are meant to be used even if there is a risk involved. Our gifts are not to be hoarded for ourselves. Jesus teaches us that no one lights a lamp and then puts it under a bushel basket. Rather, it is set "on a lampstand, and it gives light to all in the house. In the same way, let your light shine before others, so that they may see your good works and give glory to your Father in heaven" (Matthew 5:15–16).

Men and women in religious communities take a vow of chastity. Unfortunately, we tend to assume that chastity is strictly a sexual issue when, in truth, chastity deals with the appropriate sharing of ourselves with others. For religious men and women, the vow of chastity is a promise to remain celibate in order to share their gifts appropriately with all of God's people. Single people are also called to be chaste in their relationships. Married people are called to share themselves faithfully with their spouses so that they can then share themselves appropriately with their families and their communities. When we share ourselves appropriately with others according to our state in life, we are able to share our talents and gifts freely with the larger community.

My family participates in a weekly lottery. Once, when we had gathered for some family celebration, we sat around talking about what we would do with the money if we hit the jackpot someday. Most of us talked about new homes, traveling, and other luxuries. My brother John, however, seemed to think differently. "I'd become a philanthropist and give it all away," he said as we all looked at him as though he were from another planet. "I've always wanted to be a philanthropist," he said, and I realized that, indeed, he already was one. He didn't have millions to give away, but he was always so generous with what he did have. John seemed to realize that our time here on earth is short and that nothing we accumulate in this life would find its way to the next life anyway, so you might as well give it away! (JSP)

Giving Our Treasure

Our society places a great deal of value on material possessions. It is not wrong to enjoy the many wonderful things, including luxuries, that human beings have produced with their God-given talent and with God's resources. How we use these possessions, however, reveals our true attitudes and priorities. Humility reminds us that we have not earned these possessions but have been blessed with them. Our call to live as followers of Jesus challenges us to consider justice. And justice involves our consideration for others' material needs. Our Christian faith places high priority on caring for the poor.

When it comes to money, we tend to think of it as ours. An attitude of stewardship reminds us that it is only through the grace of God that we are able to earn money in the first place. As such, a Christian steward approaches money with the following attitude:

- All of our income belongs to God.

- God recognizes that we will need a large percentage of that money to provide for our own needs and the needs of our families.

- At the same time, God encourages us with faith to first show our gratitude for the gift of this money by setting aside a certain percentage of our income to give back.

In the Old Testament, the suggested amount of 10 percent, or a tithe, of one's income needs to be understood in context. Since Israel was a theocracy, this amount can be considered an income tax—a compulsory "donation" required to fund the workings of a government. Charity, on the other hand, was always considered to be a voluntary act. The New Testament never requires Christians to tithe. Rather than suggesting a percentage, the New Testament suggests an attitude of giving as expressed by St. Paul in his second letter to the Corinthians:

The point is this: the one who sows sparingly will also reap sparingly, and the one who sows bountifully will also reap bountifully. Each of you must give as you have made

up your mind, not reluctantly or under compulsion, for
God loves a cheerful giver. (2 Corinthians 9:6–7)

What does this mean for a Catholic who wants to know how much is the right amount to give? It means that, while no one can determine what percentage is proper for you, you are called to consider a percentage that is appropriate in relation to how much you have been given and what your circumstances dictate. (Average Americans give annually about 3.2 percent of their income, before taxes, to charity, according to a 2001 study by Independent Sector.) The very act of determining a percentage of your income to give back means that you are giving, not based on what is left over, but out of gratitude, based on your recognition that all your income is a gift of God. This type of giving is an act of worship, since it is giving God the best of what we have with a heart full of thanks and praise. This type of giving is an act of trust, since it is giving not out of abundance but out of need. This type of giving promotes humility, since it removes any illusion that we are giving something that is ours. Stewardship is not a matter of giving up a certain percentage of what is ours. Rather, it is a matter of recognizing that we are blessed to be able to keep a large percentage of what is God's after we've returned to him a small percentage of what already belongs to him! This kind of thinking is unlike the child whose mother brought him to church with two quarters, one in each of his hands. One, she told him, was to buy himself a candy bar at the drugstore after Mass. The other was for God. She instructed him to place that one in the collection basket at Mass. As he skipped happily at her side to church clutching his quarters, he tripped and one of the quarters fell out of his hand and rolled into a sewer. Without missing a beat, he looked up at his mother and exclaimed, "Too bad! God's quarter just fell into the sewer!"

In religious communities, men and women take a vow of poverty. This does not mean walking around in rags and being penniless. Poverty is an attitude of detachment from material goods. Men and women in vowed religious communities promise not to have personal ownership of material goods but rather to share them in community, recognizing that God has blessed them in abundant ways. In the same way, all Christians are called to live in detachment from material goods and to recognize God's abundant grace. This is not to say that material goods are bad, but our approach to them can be harmful if we are possessive. When we are detached from material goods, we are able to recognize that God's grace alone truly sustains us, allowing us to share more freely with others what treasure we do have.

I was teaching sophomores in the high school seminary about the traditional vows that men and women in religious communities take: poverty, chastity, and obedience. I asked, in general, what the young men thought of this type of lifestyle. One student quickly raised his hand and said, "It just sounds so challenging. That way of life is too difficult. I'd rather get married." Of course, I had to refrain from breaking into laughter! The notion that somehow marriage would be "easier" than religious life revealed a total lack of understanding about the sacrifices involved in marriage and, for that matter, in any committed Christian life. I proceeded to explain to the students how, if you don't think you'll practice poverty, chastity, and obedience in a marriage, you'll be in for a big surprise. The truth is, whatever lifestyle we choose, we can truly serve God and others only by detaching from material goods, appropriately sharing ourselves with others, and remaining accountable to the communities we are a part of. (JSP)

In the end, stewardship is not a program designed to support the parish—it is a way of living. We are called to share our time, talent, and treasure with the various communities of which we are a part: our families, workplaces, neighborhoods, parishes, towns, cities, and so forth. The presentation of the simple gifts of bread and wine, as well as our sacrificial financial offering, symbolizes the sacrifices we are called to make each day for the praise and glory of God's name, for our good, and for the good of all of God's holy church.

The Other Six Days of the Week

With regard to daily life, the Presentation of the Gifts invites and challenges us to

- share our time, talent, and treasure with the various communities we belong to: families, workplaces, neighborhoods, towns, cities, and so forth;

- live, work, and play with a spirit of poverty (a sense of detachment from material goods);

- live, work, and play with a spirit of obedience (a sense of accountability when it comes to how we spend our time);

- live, work, and play with a spirit of chastity (a recognition of our giftedness and a commitment to share these gifts appropriately with others);

- recognize that God's grace is enough for us and that his grace alone truly sustains us;

- live as good stewards of God's creation;

- determine an appropriate percentage of our income to give back to God, thankful for the opportunity to keep the rest for our own needs and for the needs of our families.

■ ■ ■

Like good stewards of the manifold grace of God, serve one another with whatever gift each of you has received.

1 Peter 4:10

9

We Give Thanks and Remember

The Eucharistic Prayer

I am in my fourth decade of priesthood, and I cannot begin to count the number of times I have celebrated Mass. I've celebrated Mass with thousands in attendance, and I have celebrated Mass all alone. I have been deep in prayer many times during Mass, and I have occasionally found myself so tired that I was, unfortunately, on automatic pilot. There were times I was so distracted that I stumbled over the sacred words or lost my place. And there were liturgies where I was struck silent by the awesome mystery of what was happening. Over the years I have grown in my appreciation of the Mass. It has become both the cornerstone and the apex of my prayer life. Its richness continues to unfold, surprising and moving me. I look forward to Mass, not just celebrating it, but also those times I can sit as part of a congregation when I am traveling. It remains an incredible privilege, central to all that I do and all that I am as a priest. Yet, at the same time, I am learning to grow more transparent so that not I, but the reality of what we celebrate, will be the focus. It makes no difference if there are ten people in the congregation or a thousand praying with me. It is our prayer together. A few years ago I found myself lying immobile in a hospital bed. I realized that of everything I would miss if I did not recover, I would most miss celebrating the Mass. Now when I say the words of the Eucharistic Prayer, especially the words of the institution narrative, the depth of Jesus' self-offering and the blessing of being able to pray the words he spoke fill me with awe, humility, and thanksgiving. (DJG)

F ew things frighten Catholics more than the words *changes in the Mass.* The Mass, after all, is a ritual, and rituals endure because of their comforting and unchanging nature. But the fact is, the Mass has undergone numerous changes over the ages, not the least of which were the changes implemented by the Second Vatican Council in the 1960s and most recently the translation of the 3rd Edition of the Roman Missal, implemented in Advent 2011. Without a historical perspective, we may be tempted to think that the Mass remained unchanged for more than nineteen hundred years until those changes took place. Although some of the ways in which we celebrate the Mass changed over the centuries, the essence of the Mass has remained constant. Nowhere is this truer than in the Eucharistic Prayer—the prayer that enables us to be sent forth from the Mass remembering God's great deeds, celebrating Christ's dying and rising, and believing in his presence with us now.

It would take an entire book to give a detailed history of just how the Eucharistic Prayer has evolved over the centuries. For our purposes, we will focus on the chief elements of the Eucharistic Prayer that have remained constant, especially the words and actions of Jesus at the Last Supper, when he gave us the sacred meal to celebrate as well as the sacrifice of his very self, the new Passover lamb. In addition to Jesus' words at the Last Supper, the Eucharistic Prayer has always included the prayers of the church, intercessions to the saints, remembrances of the dead, prayers for church leaders, and more.

From the fourth century on, the Eucharistic Prayer, along with the whole Mass, was prayed in Latin—the vernacular language for many in the Holy Roman Empire. Over time, however, as places of worship grew larger and the language of the people evolved and became more diversified, much of what the celebrant prayed in Latin with his back to the people was not heard by the congregation, much less understood. The increasingly passive role of the assembly, coupled with the emphasis on the actions of the priest in consecrating the bread and wine, led to some interesting and unfortunate phenomena that continue to influence our understanding of the Eucharistic Prayer.

For example, during the Middle Ages, there was a period of time when the faithful would literally run from church building to church building trying to arrive in time for the elevation—the part of the Eucharistic Prayer when the priest, with his back to the congregation, consecrated the bread (which, as the years passed, looked less and less like what was found on the dinner table) and wine by lifting them up over his head. The people waited for the bells to be rung to alert them to the sacred moment. Once it passed, they would run out in search of another church, eager to see the precise moment at which they believed bread and wine were becoming the body and blood of Jesus, as though the priest were performing a magic act to be witnessed rather than a sacred action in which to participate. Likewise, it is believed that the traditional magician's formula of saying, "hocus pocus" while performing magic is actually a mockery of the consecration of the bread and wine. In Latin, the priest prayed the words *Hoc est enim corpus meum* ("This is my body") just after consecrating the bread and wine by making a sign of the cross over the paten and chalice with his hand. To the average person, who could not speak Latin and could not hear the priest's hushed tones, these words sounded like "hocus pocus."

Because of their passive role during the Eucharistic Prayer, people often prayed private devotions, stopping and looking up only for what they felt was the most important moment in the Eucharistic Prayer—indeed in the entire liturgy—the moment of consecration. Most believed that this was accomplished solely at that moment by the priest uttering, in Latin, "This is my body" and "This is my blood" while elevating the consecrated host and wine. This belief clearly indicated a lack of understanding of Jesus' words, "Do this in memory of me" (Luke 22:19)—words that came to be wrongly understood as referring to something the priest alone was to accomplish through his power to consecrate. However, the words—"Do this in memory of me"—are addressed to all who are gathered to celebrate the Eucharist. Although the priest alone prays aloud the words of the Eucharistic Prayer, he is praying the words on behalf of, and in union with, all those gathered. The priest shares the Eucharistic Prayer with the community of believers who are worshiping together with him. At the Second Vatican Council (1962–1965), the bishops of the Catholic Church expressed this understanding in the *Constitution on the Sacred Liturgy*:

"The Church, therefore, earnestly desires that Christ's faithful, when present at this mystery of faith, should not be there as strangers or silent spectators; on the contrary, through a good understanding of the rites and prayers they should take part in the sacred action conscious of what they are doing, with devotion and full collaboration. They should be instructed by God's word and be nourished at the table of the Lord's body; they should give thanks to God; by offering the Immaculate Victim, not only through the hands of the priest, but also with him, they should learn also to offer themselves" (48).

The Eucharistic Prayer appears in several variations yet with the same principal elements. There are currently four basic Eucharistic Prayers prayed at Mass:

- Eucharistic Prayer I is also referred to as the Roman Canon since it was the only Eucharistic Prayer permitted in the Roman rite from the Council of Trent to the Second Vatican Council. Although it was inspired by a eucharistic prayer written by St. Ambrose in the fourth century, its current structure can be traced to the Mass of Pope Pius V

(1570). This prayer calls to mind the story of salvation history, beginning with the Jewish people and continuing through the apostles, saints, and martyrs whom we call upon for help in achieving our ultimate goal—union with God in heaven.

- Eucharistic Prayer II, although newly written after the Second Vatican Council, actually has its roots in a third-century eucharistic prayer written by St. Hippolytus of Rome. This prayer is beautiful in its brevity and simplicity.

- Eucharistic Prayer III imitates the pattern of Eucharistic Prayer I, although it is much shorter. The focus of this prayer is on God's saving action, calling all of God's children "scattered throughout the world" (Eucharistic Prayer III) to be united.

- Eucharistic Prayer IV, modeled on prayers from the West Syrian liturgy, uses images from Scripture—creation, the covenant, the Incarnation—to tell the story of salvation history.

In addition, special eucharistic prayers for various occasions have also been written. There are also rich traditions of liturgies and eucharistic prayers for Eastern Churches in union with Rome. No matter what form the Eucharistic Prayer takes, the principal elements provide the faithful with a clear focus of what Jesus wants us to do in his memory—namely, remember, celebrate, give thanks, and believe.

Thanksgiving and Acclamation

What do you think you will be doing for all eternity? We sometimes picture ourselves floating around on clouds doing nothing. While that may sound appealing in the short run, an eternity of such nothingness sounds more like hell than heaven. If Scripture references to eternal life are any indication, eternity will not be a passive reality but an active one. At the very least, we will be giving thanks and praise to God. The Eucharistic Prayer begins by giving us a taste of this. The priest invites us to begin our thanksgiving with the Preface dialogue:

> Priest: The Lord be with you.
> People: And with your spirit.
>
> Priest: Lift up your hearts.
> People: We lift them up to the Lord.
>
> Priest: Let us give thanks to the Lord our God.
> People: It is right and just.

Next, as the Preface continues, the priest expresses our desire to praise God. The Preface, which changes from Sunday to Sunday and from day to day, joins the prayers of the priest and the people of God with those of the angels and saints in heaven in giving thanks and praise to God. The church has numerous Prefaces, each one giving thanks and praise for particular feasts, holy days, seasons of the church year, or, more generally, for Sundays or weekdays. Some are for

weddings or funerals or other specific liturgies. Here is one
of the Prefaces used during the Easter season:

>It is truly right and just, our duty and our salvation,
>at all times to acclaim you, O Lord,
>but (on this night / on this day / in this time)
>above all
>to laud you yet more gloriously,
>when Christ our Passover has been sacrificed.
>For he is the true Lamb
>who has taken away the sins of the world;
>by dying he has destroyed our death,
>and by rising, restored our life.
>Therefore, overcome with paschal joy,
>every land, every people exults in your praise
>and even the heavenly Powers, with the angelic
>hosts,
>sing together the unending hymn of your glory,
>as they acclaim:
>Holy, Holy, Holy Lord God of hosts . . .
>>Preface I of Easter, *The Roman Missal*

The acclamation of the congregation to the Preface—the
Sanctus (Holy, Holy)—is rooted in a Jewish synagogue prayer
from the second century and is based on the song of the
angels from the sixth chapter of Isaiah.

>Holy, Holy, Holy Lord God of hosts.
>Heaven and earth are full of your glory.
>Hosanna in the highest.

Blessed is he who comes in the name of the Lord.
Hosanna in the highest.

This acclamation joins our voices with the chorus of angels in heaven who are constantly singing praise to the God of hosts (meaning the God of the armies of angels) and also echoes the cries of "Hosanna!" shouted by the crowds who welcomed Jesus into Jerusalem as their king just days before his crucifixion. The faithful then express deep reverence for the Eucharistic Prayer by placing themselves on their knees as the priest continues to express our prayers.

Invocation

Most sports fans can think of a local hero who, when called upon, always seems to come through. By doing what he or she does best, this athlete more often than not saves the team from going down to defeat. In our lives, we, too, call upon someone greater than ourselves—namely, God—to do what he does best: save us. When called upon, God always comes through. In this part of the Eucharistic Prayer, known as the *epiclesis* (Greek for "*the calling down, or invocation*"), we pray in a way that once again expresses our dependence on God. We call upon God because we know that without him we are nothing and that he alone can save us. The priest expresses our desire that by the power of the Holy Spirit, the gifts of bread and wine will become for us the body and blood of Christ and that all who receive him will be saved.

You are indeed Holy, O Lord,
and all you have created
rightly gives you praise,
for through your Son our Lord Jesus Christ,
by the power and working of the Holy Spirit,
you give life to all things and make them holy,
and you never cease to gather a people to yourself,
so that from the rising of the sun to its setting
a pure sacrifice may be offered to your name.

Therefore, O Lord, we humbly implore you:
by the same Spirit graciously make holy
these gifts we have brought to you for consecration,
that they may become the Body and Blood
of your Son our Lord Jesus Christ,
at whose command we celebrate these mysteries.
                    Eucharistic Prayer III, *The Roman Missal*

These words make it clear that the transformation of bread and wine into the body and blood of Jesus will be accomplished through the power of God and that we are fortunate to be the recipients of his saving action.

Every August, when our kids were little, my wife and I would sit down to complete the task of "synchronizing" our calendars. With school about to start, we needed to mark down significant dates in our kids' calendars, as well as our own. The overriding goal of this planning was to ensure that we could be present to our kids, especially at significant moments. Most of what a parent does can be summed up by this phrase: *being present*.

We are present to our children when they learn to walk, talk, and eventually ride a bike. We are present to them at graduations—preschool, kindergarten, eighth grade, high school, and college. We are present to them on birthdays and important holidays, at academic and extracurricular events. We are present to them when they are sick and when they get into trouble, when they achieve success and when they just want to talk. We are present to them in the ordinary moments of each day, as well as in the extraordinary moments that pop up from time to time. Through it all, we want them to know that they are not alone—that they are loved, supported, and have our approval. Children make a lot of noise about wanting many things, but ultimately, what they want is their parents' undivided attention and approval—in other words, their presence. (JSP)

Institution Narrative

When it comes to the notion of *presence,* God is the ultimate parent. Parents striving to be present to their children can look to God for the perfect example. God manifested his presence to his chosen people in the Old Testament in a burning bush, in a column of smoke by day and a pillar of fire at night, in the Ark of the Covenant, in the temple, and through countless miracles and words of assurance. Realizing our need for assurances of God's presence, God sent us his only Son, Jesus, so that we might see God's presence in the flesh. In turn, Jesus gave us the Eucharist, that he might be present to us always, even "to the end of the age" (Matthew 28:20). The Eucharist is the most perfect manifestation of God's presence to his people. The institution narrative—recalling Jesus' words and actions at the Last Supper—brings this presence to fruition.

> For on the night he was betrayed
> he himself took bread,
> and, giving you thanks, he said the blessing,
> broke the bread and gave it to his disciples, saying:

> *Take this, all of you, and eat of it,*
> *for this is my Body,*
> *which will be given up for you.*

> In a similar way, when supper was ended,
> he took the chalice,
> and, giving you thanks, he said the blessing,
> and gave the chalice to his disciples, saying:

> *Take this, all of you, and drink from it,*
> *for this is the chalice of my Blood,*
> *the Blood of the new and eternal covenant,*
> *which will be poured out for you and for many*
> *for the forgiveness of sins.*
> *Do this in memory of me.*
>   Eucharistic Prayer III, *The Roman Missal*

What were once simple bread and wine have now become the body and blood of our Savior and Messiah Jesus Christ. The church refers to this as *transubstantiation.* Jesus commanded his disciples to perpetuate his words and actions. In doing so, we come into communion with his real presence under the appearance of bread and wine. Because communion with Jesus is intimately tied together with his sacrificial death on the cross on Good Friday, the institution narrative is immediately followed by these words of the priest: "The mystery of faith." This bold statement serves as a prelude to our acclamation in the same way that the statements "The word of the Lord," "The Gospel of the Lord," "the Body of Christ," and "the Blood of Christ" serve as preludes to our acclamations of "Thanks be to God," (following the first and second Scripture readings), "Praise to you, Lord, Jesus Christ," (following the Gospel) and "Amen," (as we receive Holy Communion). We have three acclamations from which to choose, all calling to mind that Jesus died, rose again to save us, and will return for us.

> We proclaim your Death, O Lord,
> and profess your Resurrection
> until you come again.

>   Or:

> When we eat this Bread and drink this Cup,
> we proclaim your Death, O Lord,
> until you come again.

>   Or:

> Save us, Savior of the world,
> for by your Cross and Resurrection
> you have set us free.
>   Eucharistic Prayer III, *The Roman Missal*

So, indeed, Jesus is already with us. This is the presence we will share when we come forward to receive the body and blood of Christ in Holy Communion. As we leave the church, we carry this presence in the depth of our being—in our soul—and our subsequent actions help others see Jesus' presence in the world.

Remembering

We keep reminders around us all the time. We have reminder functions on our computers and cell phones that alert us to appointments. We keep calendars—paper and electronic—to try to recall all our commitments. We keep pictures of our loved ones around our work spaces and in our homes to remind us of the people we cherish. We use sticky notes to remind ourselves to pick up the kids or the dry cleaning or both. Reminders are important. In the Eucharistic Prayer, we remind ourselves once again of all the great and wonderful ways God has shown his love for us. This part of the Eucharistic Prayer, known as the *anamnesis* (from the Greek for "remembering"), prevents us from developing a short memory when it comes to our salvation.

> Therefore, O Lord, as we celebrate the memorial
> of the saving Passion of your Son,
> his wondrous Resurrection
> and Ascension into heaven [. . .]
>   Eucharistic Prayer III, *The Roman Missal*

Through remembering the past, we become aware of God's presence in the present and look forward to his continuing presence in the future.

Offering

It is human nature to reciprocate. When someone shows kindness or generosity toward us, we seek to respond in a way that shows our thanks and appreciation. We often say, "If there is anything I can do to show my appreciation, let me know." At this point in the Eucharistic Prayer, we show our appreciation for all God has done for us. We offer not only this "Bread of life and the Chalice of salvation" (Eucharistic Prayer II) but also ourselves. In essence, we tell God, "If there's anything that we can do in your name . . . "

> We offer you in thanksgiving
> this holy and living sacrifice. . . .

> May he make of us
> an eternal offering to you
>   Eucharistic Prayer III, *The Roman Missal*

This part of the Eucharistic Prayer reminds us that our offering is really a response to God's invitation. We do not offer ourselves to God to get his attention but to respond actively and willingly in appreciation for the attention he shows us.

Intercessions

During the Liturgy of the Word, we offered intercessions during the Prayer of the Faithful. In this part of the Eucharistic Prayer, we once again pray for the church and for all her members, living and dead. This is further proof that we can never pray enough and that St. Paul was serious when he told the Thessalonians to "pray without ceasing" (1 Thessalonians 5:17).

> Be pleased to confirm in faith and charity
> your pilgrim Church on earth,
> with your servant, N. our Pope, N. our Bishop,
> the Order of Bishops, all the clergy,
> and the entire people you have gained for your own.
>
> Listen graciously to the prayers of this family,
> whom you have summoned before you:
> in your compassion, O merciful Father,
> gather to yourself all your children
> scattered throughout the world.
>
> To our departed brothers and sisters
> and to all who were pleasing to you
> at their passing from this life,
> give kind admittance to your kingdom.
> There we hope to enjoy for ever the fullness of
>   your glory
> through Christ our Lord,
> through whom you bestow on the world all that is
>   good.
>
> Eucharistic Prayer III, *The Roman Missal*

Earlier in the liturgy we prayed for the needs of the world and of our community; here we pray for the church, that we might be strengthened by the Eucharist to do the work of the gospel.

Final Doxology

Have you ever heard someone else express your thoughts in the very language you would have used? When that happens, we eagerly jump in and say things like, "My sentiments exactly!" or "Ditto!" or "Thank you!" Some of us may even say "Amen!" This powerful little word is a stamp of approval. To say, "Amen" is to add your voice to a voice that spoke previously, expressing your wholehearted support, acceptance, and, indeed, ownership of what was said and/or done. The final doxology, to which we respond with a resounding "Amen!" is a powerful expression of our ownership of the entire Eucharistic Prayer. As the priest raises the consecrated Host over the chalice, he prays the following words:

> Through him, and with him, and in him,
> O God, almighty Father,
> in the unity of the Holy Spirit,
> all glory and honor is yours,
> for ever and ever.

As the Eucharistic Prayer draws to its climactic conclusion, the celebrant sums up all that we have just prayed together. Our response is not just any old amen but a thunderous one. This amen, through which we give our assent and approval of the entire Eucharistic Prayer, is a resounding, or "great," amen. This amen reminds us that the Eucharistic Prayer belongs to all of those gathered to celebrate Eucharist. This amen is an expression of ownership, allowing the faithful to confirm that the words of the Eucharistic Prayer are indeed our own words.

Amen.

The richness of the Eucharistic Prayer is even deeper than that of its history. In those few moments during the Mass, whether standing or kneeling, we witness and take part in not only what Jesus gathered with his apostles to do on Holy Thursday but in the very act of salvation that was his death on Good Friday and his resurrection on Easter Sunday. Our faith is strengthened by what we have shared, strengthened to the point of taking this presence of the risen Lord with us into the world. We are not just observers of a drama unfolding, a meal being remembered, a sacrifice offered in the past. We participate in and partake of the Eucharist in the meal of Holy Thursday, the new Passover, even as we are washed clean with the blood of the Lamb of Good Friday and redeemed by the Resurrection of Easter Sunday.

The Other Six Days of the Week

With regard to daily life, the Eucharistic Prayer invites and challenges us to

- acknowledge the presence of others, especially at home and at work;

- be present to those people we are committed to: spouse, children, parents, coworkers, friends;

- recognize God's presence in all people and in all things;

- be a person of gratitude, going out of our way to thank others for small things;

- live in gratitude, appreciative of all the blessings we have;

- bring Jesus' presence to others, especially in places where there is despair;

- remind ourselves and others of God's great love for us;

- call upon God in our times of need;

- offer our daily lives to God, striving to make holy our days at work and at home by setting aside time for God's purposes.

■ ■ ■

We speak of the presence of Christ under the appearances of bread and wine as "real" in order to emphasize the special nature of that presence. What appears to be bread and wine is in its very substance the body and blood of Christ. The entire Christ is present, God and man, body and blood, soul and divinity. While the other ways in which Christ is present in the celebration of the Eucharist are certainly not unreal, this way surpasses the others.

"The Real Presence of Jesus Christ in the Sacrament of the Eucharist:
Basic Questions and Answers"—USCCB

10

Courage and Confidence

The Lord's Prayer

For years, on my way to and from work, I passed by her outside the train station. I didn't know her name, but for some unknown reason I thought of her as "Annie." Annie was homeless. She was probably in her sixties and stood no more than five feet tall. And that's precisely what she did: she stood. She stood in the same place outside the train station day in and day out, even during the coldest Chicago winters. In a frail voice, she pleaded with the thousands of passersby, "Please help me. Please help me. Please help me. . . ." I tried to help her as often as possible, as do many other folks. I didn't know what her circumstances were, but she returned to the same spot every day, seemingly confident and trusting that she had chosen the best place to stand in order to ask for and receive help. Eventually, I found myself thinking about Annie when I prayed the Lord's Prayer. It's a relatively short prayer, and it's easy to rattle off the words without thinking of their meaning. But I realized that I could learn something from Annie about praying the Lord's Prayer. I could stand before the Lord, vulnerable yet confident, and offer this prayer, which in essence says, "Please help me." (JSP)

We leave Mass with confidence—not in ourselves but in our God, who works through us. We go with a sense of surrender, letting go of our own will and desire to control, and opening up to the will of God—allowing God's power to reign. We go emptied of our own agenda and filled with the Lord's. We go with a sense of courage, realizing that we will encounter evil, but confident that we will be delivered from it. We are brought to this point through the Lord's Prayer. It reminds and teaches us to live according to the words that Jesus himself learned and then taught us: "Thy will be done."

Priest: At the Savior's command
and formed by divine teaching,
we dare to say:

Our Father, who art in heaven,
hallowed be thy name;
thy kingdom come,
thy will be done
on earth as it is in heaven.
Give us this day our daily bread,
and forgive us our trespasses,
as we forgive those who trespass against us;
and lead us not into temptation,
but deliver us from evil.

Four simple words: "Thy will be done." And yet these are among the hardest words to utter. To say, "Thy will be done," is to surrender. That's something that we don't do very readily. This world teaches us to fight for control, to win at all costs, to never give in. TV reality shows suggest that the key to survival is the ability to exert one's will over that of the other contestants.

So, does it make us weak to say, "Thy will be done"?

On the contrary, it is the only thing that can truly make us strong, for the simple reason that God's will is the driving force of the universe. Conspiring with God's will is the ultimate strategy for strength. Standing in the way of God's will is the ultimate folly. Everything that we have done in the Mass up to this point has revolved around our realization that God's will is the correct course of action. The Introductory Rites told us that we are not independent agents who can follow our own will as we please. The Penitential Act has reminded us that when we do not follow God's will, we enter into sin. The Liturgy of the Word has proclaimed to us that it is God's plan to bring us salvation. The Prayer of the Faithful has challenged us to rely on God's will in specific areas of our lives where we are in need. The Presentation of the Gifts has encouraged us that to trust in God's will is to trust in his abundance. The Eucharistic Prayer that we have just prayed has reminded us that because he followed God's will, Jesus overcame death and is present with us now. As we strive to become more like Jesus, the next logical step is to pray in the words that he used and that he taught us: "Thy will be done."

Many times, pastors have to make tough decisions. I found myself in such a position, having to fire an employee whose parents were lifelong parishioners. They were extremely hurt and very angry with me. So every Sunday they would sit in church and look at me in a way I perceived as hostile. After a few weeks of feeling guilty, I started to get angry with them. Because of my duty to respect privacy and confidentiality, I was not free to tell them what had transpired. So to them I was the villain. Their presence in the congregation became very distracting to me. It's hard to minister to people when they disagree with you or are hurt by you. You pray over the decision, you take action, and when anger gets in the way of understanding, you feel very much alone. I mentioned this to my spiritual director. Her advice was simple. Every time I saw them, and every time I thought about them, instead of thinking angry thoughts, I should pray an Our Father. I smiled at her suggestion and filed it away under "that won't work." Still, I tried it. And after a few times, something melted inside me. I walked up to them and said, "Let's talk." They both lit up and said, "That's what we've been waiting for you to suggest." We worked everything out. I have since given this suggestion to a lot of people who come to me experiencing such conflict. When we ask for God's will to be done, we let ourselves let go. When we ask to be forgiven as we forgive others, we give ourselves a task to do. When Jesus' words become ours, especially at Mass, just before communion, we compel ourselves to act. (DJG)

To surrender is a frightening proposition. We tend to equate surrender with losing and with weakness. And yet, ironically, to surrender is one of the greatest feats of strength one can perform. To surrender is to let go of what we desire, in return for what is good for us. St. Paul taught that surrender to God's will—the act of faith—is the very act that justifies us, meaning that it sets us right with God. St. Paul believed that the supposed weakness of surrender is the only thing that makes it possible for us to become strong in Jesus.

And yet, we struggle with the words *thy will be done.* If you find them difficult to utter, take comfort—you are in good company. Throughout biblical history, men and women have had trouble saying these four words.

- Adam and Eve knew that it was God's will that they not eat the fruit of the tree of the knowledge of good and evil, but they did so anyway.

- Cain knew that it was God's will that he not kill his brother Abel, but Cain did so anyway.

- The Hebrews knew that building and worshiping a golden calf was against God's will, but they did so anyway.

- David knew that it was against God's will for him to kill Uriah so that he could have Bathsheba to himself, but he did so anyway.

- Jonah knew that it was God's will that he go and preach to Nineveh, but he initially chose to ignore God's call anyway.

- Peter knew that it was God's will that he follow Jesus, and yet he denied even knowing him.

And the list goes on. St. Paul summarizes this human tendency when he writes, "I do not do the good I want, but the evil I do not want is what I do" (Romans 7:19).

At the other end of the spectrum, biblical history provides role models of people who said yes to the will of God and thus enjoyed the fullness of his love and grace.

- Abraham and Sarah said, "Thy will be done," and gave birth to a great nation.

- Moses said, "Thy will be done," and led that great nation out of slavery and into freedom.

- Ruth said, "Thy will be done," and set an example for committed family love.

- Jonah came to his senses, said, "Thy will be done," and not only saw daylight but led a corrupt city to repentance.

- Joseph said, "Thy will be done," and took Mary to be his wife.

- Mary said, "Thy will be done," and became the Mother of God and the first disciple of Jesus, a role model of faith for all believers.

Jesus, of course, is the ultimate example of what it means to live according to God's will. Before Jesus began his ministry, he was led by the Spirit into the desert, where he grappled with the temptation to follow his own will instead of the will of the Father. Instead of turning stone into bread, Jesus chose to follow God's will. Likewise, in the Garden of Gethsemane, Jesus came face-to-face with temptation, wondering if it might be possible to follow his own will instead of accepting the suffering that awaited him. It is this very temptation that Níkos Kazantzákis focused on in his classic novel *The Last Temptation of Christ*. The story portrays what might have been if Jesus had said, "My will be done," instead of "Thy will be done." If Jesus had followed his own will, he might have gone on to live a long life with a wife and children and a career as a carpenter. While there is nothing wrong with such a life, the point is that Jesus had become fully aware of his gifts and of his relationship with the Father. To have followed his own will would have been a betrayal of his true calling. The Father's will was calling Jesus to a different path—one that would bring salvation to all people. Instead of focusing on his own desires, Jesus chose to offer his life for the good of others. He chose to utter, "Yet not what I want but what you want" (Matthew 26:39).

The extent to which we follow God's will cannot be measured solely in terms of how outwardly dramatic our choices appear. Jesus knew that following God's will and remaining faithful to his calling would result in certain death at the hands of unbelievers. For many of us, God's will is that we become good carpenters—or construction workers, or lab technicians, or dental hygienists, or librarians. This does not mean that our calling is any less crucial to God's purposes for this world. While perhaps not outwardly dramatic, a young mom's call to work a part-time job while raising a family is no less crucial to God's will. Neither is a middle-aged man's call to enter into counseling to save his marriage of thirty-plus years, or a college student's call to volunteer weekly in the soup kitchen while juggling eighteen credit hours. A pastor may not become famous for dedicating several afternoons per week to preparing the Sunday homily, yet his faithfulness to this task in the midst of late nights attending parish meetings and consoling parishioners at wake services is a holy example of following God's call and will. God calls us according to our gifts, talents, and abilities to practice living out the words *thy will be done* in a variety of settings. Jesus knew that his calling was to take him beyond what we consider an ordinary life. In doing so, however, Jesus showed us how even the ordinary is transformed into the extraordinary by the power of these four words: *Thy will be done.*

Throughout Christian history, the saints and mystics have taught us over and over that discipleship is about surrender. We often strive to "add" Jesus into our lives as if adding some whipped cream to a sundae. Richard Rohr, the well-known Franciscan speaker and author, explains that spirituality is not about adding things on but about subtraction. When we remove the clutter in our lives (as we attempt to do each Lent), we create space to recognize Jesus' abiding presence. Likewise, we sometimes decide that we will devote a certain section of our lives to Jesus as if setting aside one room in our home to use as office space. C. S. Lewis explained, however, that faith is about giving ourselves entirely to Jesus:

> The Christian way is very different: harder, and easier. Christ says "Give me All. I don't want so much of your time and so much of your money and so much of your work: I want You. I have not come to torment your natural self, but to kill it. No half-measures are any good. I don't want to cut off a branch here and

a branch there, I want to have the whole tree down. I don't want to drill the tooth, or crown it, or stop it, but to have it out. Hand over the whole natural self, all the desires which you think are innocent as well as the ones you think wicked—the whole outfit. I will give you a new self instead. In fact, I will give you Myself: My own will shall become yours. (C. S. Lewis, *Mere Christianity*)

In essence, the Lord's Prayer is our "declaration of dependence." This does not come easy to those of us from the United States, which was founded on a Declaration of Independence. We Americans treasure our independence and try to teach our young to become independent. We don't consider dependency a virtue. Our forefathers laid down their lives to break away from a king. And now, here we are, in the Lord's Prayer, praying, "Thy kingdom come, thy will be done." And yet, it is this declaration of dependence—this surrender to the will of God—that enables us to truly be free.

But just what is this will of God that we are surrendering to? We hear people say, "It's God's will" when they attempt to explain away suffering. "Why did he/she have to die?" "Why did I have to lose my job?" "Why did I have to get cancer?" "Why did my marriage fail?" Despite the best of intentions, those who respond to these pleas for help (they are really not questions at all but rather, expressions of grief) with "It's God's will" are doing more harm than good. God never wills the suffering of people. While it is true that in early biblical writings, the people of Israel often saw suffering as a part of God's will that would lead them to repentance, the overall tide of Scripture flows in the direction of understanding God's will as one of fullness of life for his children. God's will can be summed up in the following passage from the prophet Jeremiah:

―――――

Surely I know the plans I have for you, says the Lord, plans for your welfare and not for harm, to give you a future with hope. (Jeremiah 29:11)

―――――

I went to a Jesuit high school, St. Ignatius College Prep, in Chicago. While the campus has grown since the late 1970s when I attended, the original building, which survived the Chicago fire a century before, remains at 1076 West Roosevelt Road. Above the doors are the words *Ad Majorem Dei Gloriam*, Latin meaning "to the greater glory of God." The founder of the Jesuit order, St. Ignatius of Loyola, coined this phrase out of his conviction that fullness of life was achieved by recognizing that "the kingdom, the power, and the glory" belong to no one but God. St. Ignatius believed that our role in life is to direct attention not to ourselves but to the glory of God. This Jesuit motto, recalling the words of St. Ignatius, is often summed up with the initials AMDG. Although I studied Latin during those years, I can't honestly say that I've retained a lot of it. However, after viewing those four words every day for four years, I've had a hard time shaking them. Sure enough, twenty years later, when I had my first opportunity to select a password to retrieve voice mail at the office where I worked, the first thing that popped into my head was the initials

AMDG. While it's true that now the whole world knows how to retrieve my phone messages, it is worth it for me to remember each and every day that what I do is not for my own glory, but for the greater glory of God. (JSP)

Priest: Deliver us, Lord, we pray, from every evil,
graciously grant peace in our days,
that, by the help of your mercy,
we may be always free from sin
and safe from all distress,
as we await the blessed hope
and the coming of our Savior, Jesus Christ.

People: For the kingdom,
the power and the glory are yours
now and for ever.

The greatest temptation, indeed, is to believe that glory belongs to us. The greatest temptation is to believe that "my will be done" will bring us fullness of life and be the answer to our prayers. To say, "My will be done," is to act as if we are lord or lady of the kingdom and that others operate under our reign. The Lord's Prayer teaches us to surrender to the will of the one true Lord and to proclaim, "The kingdom, the power, and the glory are yours, now and forever." When we pray, "Thy will be done," we open wide our lives to God's reign, surrendering our tight hold on life and our desire to control things. When we say that "the kingdom, the power, and the glory" belong to God alone, we become like John the Baptist, who, by saying, "He must increase, but I must decrease" (John 3:30) paved the way for the King of glory to reign. When we recognize that God's saving will reigns, we become like Mary, who, by saying, "Here am I, the servant of the Lord; let it be with me according to your word" (Luke 1:38) made the birth of the Messiah possible. Mary is the model for true discipleship because she deflects all glory and honor away from herself and instead "magnifies the Lord" (Luke 1:46).

In Jesus, we come to a new understanding of the word *power.* For most of the world, power is something that is used to coerce and control people. Jesus, on the other hand, showed us that God's power can never be separated from his will to save. God's power is shown through Jesus' miracles, but never for display purposes or to bully others. The power that Jesus shows in healing the blind and the lame, in calming the storm at sea, and in raising the dead is never to draw attention to himself but to the saving presence of God in the people's midst. It is the greatest of ironies that the symbol of Christian power and glory is the image of Jesus crucified. We look to the image of one who is broken and vulnerable, and rejoice in the power of salvation. If we take the Lord's Prayer to heart, we find that we are praying subversive words—words that refute the powers that be in our world for the power that comes to us only when we allow ourselves to become vulnerable.

To live for the greater glory of God is to embrace humility. (Remember the Penitential Act?) It is to reject the selfish request of the mother of James and John, who asks Jesus if her sons can have the choicest seats in the kingdom of heaven. Jesus' response is to ask them if they can drink from the same cup that he will drink from, meaning make the same commitment that he will make (see Matthew 20:22). Shortly after the apostles argue among themselves about who is the greatest (see Mark 9:33–37), Jesus draws attention to the children being brought to him and tells his disciples that unless they become like children, they have no place in the kingdom of heaven (Mark 10:15). What does this mean? Are we to forget our adult responsibilities and frolic about like children? Of course not. Jesus is telling us to assume the spiritual attitude that every child has, which is one of dependence.

Dependence is beneficial when the one we are dependent on is stronger than we are. To be like a child before God is to realize that God is stronger than we are and that we are in need of his protection. Like Frodo Baggins (in J.R.R. Tolkien's *The Lord of the Rings*) who takes comfort and courage in knowing that Samwisc Gamgee is always at his side, we are finally able to move about without fear, knowing that no threat is too big. It is no coincidence that right after we pray the Lord's Prayer, the priest prays that we will be "safe from all distress." Distress or anxiety results whenever we face something or someone that we feel ill equipped to deal with. When we pray that God's will be done and acknowledge that all power belongs to God alone, we have no more reason to be anxious or distressed. And when we are not distressed, we are capable of hope and are filled with peace—the peace of Christ that we now prepare to share with one another and with the world.

The Other Six Days of the Week

With regard to daily life, the Lord's Prayer invites and challenges us to

- stop trying to be in control of life, surrendering instead to God's will;

- live with a childlike attitude, acknowledging that we are dependent on God;

- do all things for the greater glory of God;

- live with humility;

- spread hope based on our confidence in the Father;

- encounter powerful forces, knowing that we will be delivered from them and still be at peace;

- recognize true power as service to God, not power over people.

■ ■ ■

Thy will be done on earth as it is in Heaven
grant us the grace to find all our joy
in wanting You alone,
in desiring You alone,
and in thinking of You alone.
Grant that by denying ourselves always
and in all things,
we may find light and life
in obeying Your good, acceptable, perfect Will.
I will what You will.
I will it because You will it.
I will as You will it.
I will it as long as You will it.
Perish our thoughts and desires
if they are not purely
from You, for You, and in You.

St. Julian Eymard (from the Our Father,
paraphrased by St. Julian Eymard)

11

Let Peace Begin with Me

The Sign of Peace

One of my favorite vacation memories is when Joanne and I took our kids Mike and Amy to Mackinac Island in Michigan for a few days one summer when they were little. The weather was perfect, and we set out to ride bikes around the island. After about half an hour of pedaling, we had left the crowds behind and found ourselves on the other side of the island, staring at the most beautiful vista of water and blue skies. We stopped for a rest and simply took in the beauty. For one of the rare moments of our lives together, all four of us were speechless. Amy, who was about ten years old at the time, finally broke the silence when she said in a dreamy voice, "This is like heaven . . . it's so peaceful." It occurred to me that she was not only referring to the quiet and the beauty but to the fact that all four of us were together and everything seemed just right. Peace has more to do with being together with others "the way it should be" than it does with simply being alone and quiet. (JSP)

When we "go in peace," we carry with us the peace of Christ. We go with a commitment to live in peace with one another and to work for peace. We go knowing that communion with God is possible only when peace reigns in our hearts. It is through the sign of peace that we are reminded that, ultimately, peace comes from our communion with Jesus. It is a foretaste of what is possible.

As the conflict in Vietnam grew more and more divisive across America in the 1960s and early 1970s, the antiwar movement locked on to a symbol of protest: the word *peace,* accompanied by holding up two fingers forming a V. Eventually, just flashing those fingers symbolized a position against the war. There is some irony in the fact that this was the same symbol for victory that Winston Churchill used so effectively during World War II. Like most symbols, it could be incredibly powerful. A famous photograph of activist-priest Fr. Daniel Berrigan shows him handcuffed and smiling as he is being led away by dour-faced federal marshals. He is flashing a shackled peace sign. But symbols may grow insipid. On the 1960s television show *Laugh-In,* a bejeweled Sammy Davis Jr. used the same symbol as a kind of "hip" greeting. By the time President Richard Nixon began to flash the peace sign with both hands, arms raised over his head as he boarded his presidential helicopter or Air Force One, the symbol had lost most of its original meaning and force.

During the liturgy, immediately following the Lord's Prayer and just before the congregation comes forward to receive communion, we are all invited to share in a sign of Christ's peace. It is essential that this sign of peace be perceived as more than a gesture or a political—or even a theological—statement. Likewise, it is much more than a social greeting. We have just completed a beautiful and intimate prayer to our God, given to us by Jesus, in which we ask for what we need, just as a child trustingly asks a parent. After the Lord's Prayer, there follows a natural transition: having offered this prayer of surrender and vulnerability, we now take our open hands and open arms and embrace our neighbors. The priest invites us to do so with one of the only prayers in the Mass that is directed specifically to Jesus.

> Lord Jesus Christ,
> who said to your Apostles:
> Peace I leave you, my peace I give you,
> look not on our sins,
> but on the faith of your Church,
> and graciously grant her peace and unity
> in accordance with your will.
> Who live and reign for ever and ever.
> Amen.

The priest then exchanges a verbal greeting of peace with the assembly before he or the deacon invites us to share a sign of peace with one another:

> Priest: The peace of the Lord be with you always.

> All: And with your spirit.

> Priest or deacon: Let us offer each other the sign
> of peace.

When I was growing up in our Italian household, everyone in the family was greeted with a kiss when they came in, and everyone was given a kiss when they left. Relatives directly from Italy were a little more formal, giving a kiss on both cheeks. With the rest of us it was always more informal. To this day it hasn't changed. In fact, when there is a large gathering, say Christmas or Easter, we give ourselves an extra twenty minutes before our departure time to start the round of kisses. Sometimes it takes so long that the first ones kissed need another one before we go out the door. Guests watch us in wonder. But it is second nature to us, from the youngest to the eldest. No matter how well or how poorly we got along that day, no matter what issues we may have argued about or what family matters we may have discussed, we bind ourselves together with our good-bye kisses. I am comforted that the last thing I did with my mother before she died was to kiss her. Her response was to blow a kiss to all the family gathered around her and tell us how much she loved us. It's no wonder that St. Paul instructed Christians to greet one another "with a holy kiss" (Romans 16:16). (DJG)

We turn to Jesus at this point in the liturgy as a reminder that in just a moment we will come forward to receive Christ's body and blood. It should be noted that from the earliest days of the church, Christians greeted one another with the "kiss of peace." This greeting indicated that all differences were put aside. Our common belief in Jesus and the very presence of Jesus in our hearts bring us together and hold us together. This sacred kiss heals, bonds, and strengthens our relationships with one another. Over the centuries this kiss of peace was formalized into a liturgical gesture for the ordained, who turned to one another, grasped arms, and nodded to the left and right shoulder of the other. "Pax tecum," in Latin. Peace to you.

When the sign of peace was reintroduced to the liturgy after the Second Vatican Council, there were some who felt it was a disruption. How could we go from respectful silence to this moment of reaching out, kissing, hugging, and shaking hands, often with strangers in the pews around us? Some felt this was disrespectful. This reaction was understandable from people who had been taught, in effect, that the Mass was a private devotion. Understood in its proper context, the sign of peace is not an interruption of the Mass but is a beautiful and important prelude for the reception of Holy Communion. It again points us in the direction of what will happen immediately after we leave the church at the conclusion of the liturgy.

The sign of peace is needed to help us recognize that the communion we are about to enter into is not only with God but with our neighbors. The powerful intimacy of the Eucharist is foreshadowed by the intimacy of our offering Christ's peace to one another. As the hymn challenges us, "Let peace begin with me / Let this be the moment now." Let Christ's peace take away our fears and anxieties, just as it did when the risen Christ entered the upper room where the disciples had locked themselves. "Peace be with you," he said to the disciples, and so, by virtue of our baptism, we are commissioned to share that peace with all others.

We are reminded of the admonition given to us by Jesus: "So when you are offering your gift at the altar, if you remember that your brother or sister has something against you, leave your gift there before the altar and go; first be reconciled with your brother or sister, and then come and offer your gift" (Matthew 5:23–24). Now is that time. We share the intimacy of Christ's peace, leaving arguments and fears behind us before we can share in the Eucharist. But we also commit ourselves to take with us, when we leave the church after Mass, that peace found most deeply in the presence of Christ.

This is a difficult challenge for us to grasp. More than once we've seen people (including ourselves) who haven't even left the church parking lot before losing their temper at another driver, or we hear a group of people gossiping about someone as they enjoy a parish breakfast after Mass. Something was left behind or lost—the commitment to be peacemakers.

We know that peace is more than just an absence of war or violence. It is a palpable reality that must be shared. It becomes a way of looking at our world through the eyes of faith. Ultimately, peace is what results when God's will and the human heart become one. It is what results when God's will is done on earth as it is in heaven. It is what results when heaven and earth are joined. This is why the angels sang, "Glory to God in the highest and peace to all people on earth" when Jesus was born—because heaven and earth were finally joined. It is the reason we place a star or an angel atop our Christmas trees and a crèche beneath them to show that heaven and earth are now connected through the incarnation of Jesus. The result is peace. Peace involves the ability to put everything into perspective and to respond to life in ways that bring out the best in others. It is an aura that surrounds us and also attracts people to us like boats to a safe harbor. Peace works toward a more just society with more loving relationships, first between ourselves and Jesus and then with others.

The peace of Christ is much more than a symbol, which can and usually does lose its meaning, and much deeper than a sign, which often trivializes what it is trying to represent. This peace is a reality toward which we work unceasingly. The sign of peace both represents and begins that hard work to which we will commit ourselves when the liturgy is over. To extend the sign of peace to others is to offer the profound wish that heaven and earth may be joined in their hearts.

In the Sermon on the Mount, Jesus says, "Blessed are the peacemakers, for they will be called children of God" (Matthew 5:9). It is interesting that Jesus needed to teach those following him what it meant to share peace. It wasn't until many chapters later in Matthew 14:13–21 that Jesus fed those same hungry folks who followed him around and listened to him. Did they finally know better what it meant to be peacemakers? Were they finally starting to show it in their actions? Perhaps they did when, in the sharing of the blessed bread, each took only what he or she needed. No one hoarded any, and so there were basketfuls left over.

Ultimately, peace is that generosity of spirit that puts the needs of others before our own. We will need to be strengthened in order to do that. So, in sharing Christ's peace, we move ourselves to that solemn moment when we take Jesus into our hearts in the sharing of his body and blood.

The Other Six Days of the Week

With regard to daily life, the sign of peace invites and challenges us to

- leave at the altar our angers and negative thoughts about others;

- work to find time for peace and serenity in our hearts;

- work to be peacemakers with our families, in our neighborhoods, at our workplaces, in our communities, and in the world;

- be less judgmental of others;

- be active in support of civil causes that promote peace;

- take part in the political process of our land;

- monitor the tone of the messages and statements we make in social media.

■ ■ ■

Peace Prayer of Saint Francis

Lord, make me an instrument of your peace:
where there is hatred, let me sow love;
where there is injury, pardon;
where there is doubt, faith;
where there is despair, hope;
where there is darkness, light;
where there is sadness, joy.

St. Francis of Assisi

12

God Alone Sustains Us

Holy Communion

I once had the opportunity to entertain a priest visiting from Ireland, and when I found out he liked ice cream, I took him to a place that advertises thirty-one flavors of it. Either he didn't catch on or he was employing some of that sly Irish humor when he approached the counter and asked the young lady who was standing in front of a huge sign advertising all thirty-one flavors, "What kind of flavors would you be having?" The look on the girl's face was absolutely priceless as she tried to determine whether or not he was serious. Her look of disbelief gradually turned to one of frustration as the priest took a seeming eternity to decide which of the thirty-one flavors he wanted, asking question after question about each of them. To top it off, she couldn't understand him when he finally asked for "hot foodge!" I laughed at the whole incident but couldn't help but think that one of the things that complicate life nowadays is the wide variety of choices we have for everything. It's nice to have options. But sometimes the vast array of choices available to us can cause us to lose sight of what really satisfies us. (JSP)

W e are able to "go in peace" because we have entered into communion with God and with one another. The Eucharistic Prayer and the sharing of Christ's peace lead us directly into partaking of the Eucharist itself, what we call Holy Communion. Through this participation, we are embraced by God and thus strengthened to go in peace.

Did you know that the obligation of going to Mass on Sunday and receiving communion has just as much to do with the first commandment as it does the third commandment? It's true. Surprised? Although the third commandment instructs us to keep the Lord's Day holy, going to Mass is only one of the ways that we do that. In addition to worship, we keep the Lord's Day holy by refraining from unnecessary work, maintaining "the joy proper to the Lord's Day," performing "works of mercy," and relaxing the "mind and body" (*Catechism of the Catholic Church*, 2185).

The first commandment, on the other hand, says the following:

===

I am the LORD your God, who brought you out of the land of Egypt, out of the house of slavery; you shall have no other gods before me. You shall not make for yourself an idol, whether in the form of anything that is in heaven above, or that is on the earth beneath, or that is in the

water under the earth. You shall not bow down to them or
worship them (Exodus 20:2–5).

―――――――――――

God is telling us that the foundation of the Ten
Commandments is the realization that God alone is our
source of fulfillment. Nothing else! No one else! Not our
looks, money, possessions, status, friends, family, geographi-
cal location, popularity, power, or abilities.

God alone.

That's what going to Mass and receiving communion
are all about. From the moment we enter the church building for Mass, we are being invited and challenged to realize
that God alone sustains us. Challenged, because throughout
the rest of the week we are being subtly seduced with myriad
messages promising that something else can or will sustain
us. Little by little, we can fall prey to those who tell us we will
find happiness if we buy specific brands of clothes, drive a
certain make of car, maintain an optimal weight, have a flaw-
less body shape, live in a sought-after area of town or in an
ostentatious home, have a high-powered job, make a salary
we can brag about, enjoy an enviable amount of sex, achieve
a tremendous level of popularity, and wield ample amounts
of power.

The message of the Eucharist, on the other hand, is
very clear: at our deepest level, we are incapable of sustain-
ing ourselves. The message of the Eucharist is the message of
Ash Wednesday: without God, we are dust, incapable of sus-
taining ourselves. Once a year, on Ash Wednesday, we need
that message to smack us right between the eyes as a wake-up

call. Every Sunday, when we receive communion, we are reminded that, although there's nothing inherently wrong with all of those things, when we trust any of them to satisfy and sustain us, we have slipped off track. We have separated ourselves from our true source—the God who loves us.

There's a reason why this is the first commandment. When a scribe asked Jesus what the first (meaning "greatest") commandment was, Jesus responded by summarizing the first commandment:

The first is, "Hear, O Israel: the Lord our God, the Lord is one; you shall love the Lord your God with all your heart, and with all your soul, and with all your mind, and with all your strength." (Mark 12:29–30)

On another occasion, when a rich young man asked Jesus what he needed to do to achieve eternal life, Jesus told him to sell everything he owned, give the money to the poor, and follow Jesus (Matthew 19:16–26). Jesus was not saying that we all need to sell our possessions to achieve eternal life. He was challenging this particular man, who clearly thought that his money was his source of fulfillment, to realize that God alone was the source. When the church teaches us that the Eucharist is the "source and summit" of our lives (*Catechism of the Catholic Church,* 1324), it is reminding us that God alone, who is present in the Eucharist, is our source of fulfillment. When we live by the first commandment, the rest of the commandments fall into place. If we truly recognize that God alone is the source of our fulfillment, then we will honor his name, keep the Sabbath day holy, and love our neighbors as ourselves (the fourth through tenth commandments).

Receiving communion is the ultimate acknowledgment that God is our source, is everything that we need.

> A coworker once referred to me as a "grazer" because I am always grazing on snacks at work. I can't help it . . . I am always hungry. My desk drawer is like a little snack shop. I've got a stash of crackers, granola bars, raisins, pretzels, bran flakes, and other assorted goodies to tide me over as the day goes on. Now that I'm old enough to carry an AARP card, I need to pay attention to what I'm eating, knowing that I can't burn off the calories the way I used to. Although I'm always hungry, I have to eat the right foods lest the calories pile on. There are lots of foods that I would love to snack on: cookies, donuts, jelly beans, and so on. These foods would satisfy my hunger but ultimately would do more harm than good. (JSP)

It is no accident that the first temptation Jesus faced in the desert was to satisfy his hunger by turning stones to bread. It is also no accident that Jesus chose food and drink to communicate his presence to us. Jesus knows that no matter how much food and drink we take in, we will still eventually grow hungry and thirsty. In the same way, no matter how much we try to fill the emptiness we feel within, we will always be spiritually hungry and thirsty—a reality that singer Bruce Springsteen expressed so passionately: "everybody's got a hungry heart!" The question comes down to this: What will we choose to satisfy this insatiable hunger and unquenchable thirst? We have many options. There are many things in life that will bring us satisfaction in the short term. The problem is that many of these choices are unhealthy. The first commandment teaches us that God alone is the "food" of choice.

In my teaching years I was prone to catch every bug and virus my students did. One particularly bad year, I was so run-down that the doctor threatened to hospitalize me by the end of the week if I wasn't doing better. Fearing that, I went home to my parents' house to crash and rest. When I walked in, my dad saw how bad I looked and said that no matter what was wrong, Mom would take care of me. Mom saw me, and her eyes opened wide. She repeated his words, telling me she would take care of me and not to worry. I realized then how truly bad I must look. Before long there was a feast set before me. My appetite, long dormant, was quickly restored. "Eat," Mom commanded. She told me that there was iron in the rapini greens, potassium in the tomato sauce, and protein in the steak. After the meal, I went to bed and slept for fifteen hours. I was awakened for another feast, which my mom assured me would cure me. "Eat," she insisted. Again I ate and I slept. I was back in the classroom before I expected to be. And when I saw the doctor at the end of the week, he remarked that I looked 100 percent better. And I felt that way. The Eucharist is there for us no matter what ails us. It is not just for the healthy. It is especially useful to bring us back to the Lord if we've found ourselves stricken with any spiritual malady. (DJG)

In his book *The Journey of Desire,* John Eldredge explains that ultimately, when it comes to satisfying our inner hunger or desire, we have three choices. We can choose to ignore or repress our inner desire or, in his words, to "be dead." We often wrongly assume that this is the message of Christianity—the call to repress all desire. A second path traveled by all too many of us is the choice to "be addicted." In our attempts to satisfy our inner hunger and overcome that inner ache, we can easily become addicted to anything from which we derive temporary satisfaction. Finally, according to Eldredge, the third, and only viable choice for Christians, is to "be alive and thirsty" or, for our purposes here, alive and hungry.

Eldredge asserts that "the Christian is called to the life of 'holy longing,'" borrowing a phrase from Ronald Rolheiser's book on Christian spirituality, *The Holy Longing.* C. S. Lewis used a similar image when he talked about an *inconsolable longing* for "we know not what." In essence, we are striving to satisfy an insatiable hunger. Repression and addiction simply exacerbate our inner hunger and cause damage to our health. God alone can satisfy the desires of the heart, allowing us to "be alive and thirsty." Communion is our act of directing all our desire to God and God's act of offering us the bread of life and the cup of eternal salvation. It is no wonder that we are blessed to be called to this extraordinary meal!

> Priest: Behold the Lamb of God,
> behold him who takes away the sins of the world.
> Blessed are those called to the supper of the
>   Lamb.

> People: Lord, I am not worthy
> that you should enter under my roof,
> but only say the word
> and my soul shall be healed.

We are humbly and profoundly grateful to receive this invitation. Our response echoes the words of the centurion who expressed his deep appreciation to Jesus for offering to enter his home to cure his servant: "Lord, I am not worthy to have you come under my roof; but only speak the word, and my servant will be healed" (Matthew 8:8). When we come to recognize that God alone can heal us—can satisfy our hunger and thirst—our lives find balance. St. Augustine famously said, "Our hearts are restless, Lord, until they rest in you." We come to recognize that this inner restlessness is ultimately a desire for God. This same recognition leads us to overcome the temptation to allow anything else to usurp God's role as the source of our satisfaction.

As children, we may have developed an expectation that going to communion would be like Popeye eating his spinach and experiencing a sudden transformation. As we mature, however, we learn that such an approach treats communion as if it is a commodity and we are consumers. Naturally, like all consumers, we would expect immediate gratification. We learn, however, that the Eucharist is not a commodity. It's an embrace. Not a momentary embrace, but a lifelong one.

Through our reception of communion, we are embraced by God, who heals and satisfies our inner ache. We speak of receiving the real presence of Jesus in Holy Communion. What does this mean? In the New Testament, the word *body* (*soma* in Greek) refers to the very person or being, which is more than a physical body or flesh (*sarx* in Greek). In Hebrew, however, there is no specific or distinct word for *body*. A living being was not thought of as a person within a body; the body and the person were seen as one and the same. In other words, when Jesus offers us his body, he is offering us his being, his very personhood. Likewise, in Jewish thought, blood was believed to be the very life of a living being. This is why the consumption of blood was prohibited—life is strictly God's domain. When Jesus offers us his blood, he invites us to "consume" his very life. In essence, to receive the Eucharist is to be consumed with Jesus. Our being and life come into communion with Jesus' being and life. The real presence of Jesus means that we believe we are truly receiving Jesus' actual being and life, not just fondly recalling them.

At the same time, our reception of communion is an embrace not only of God but of our neighbors as well. Communion is not a "me and God" experience. The fact that we eat from the same table and drink from one cup is a powerful expression of our communion with one another. We don't normally sit at a dinner table with just anyone. To share a table is to enter into relationship with others. We don't normally drink from the same cup that someone else is drinking from unless we have an intimate relationship with that person. So we are, in a sense, becoming intimate with those who share the cup of communion. Our communion with God is thus fulfilled by loving our brothers and sisters. Communion compels us to recognize the presence of God not only in the consecrated bread and wine but also in the flesh of those we will encounter each and every day. God sent us his only Son, Jesus, to become flesh, because he "so loved the world" (John 3:16). By receiving communion, we commit ourselves to God's love for the world—a love that desires justice for all people. Our worship of God, through the celebration of the Eucharist, is meaningless unless it points us in the direction of our neighbors. This is why Jesus told the scribe who asked about the first (greatest) commandment that the second (next greatest) commandment was this: "'You shall love your neighbor as yourself.' There is no other commandment greater than these" (Mark 12:31).

In his book *The Liberation of the Laity,* theologian Paul Lakeland reminds us that "we know God only by knowing how God acts." We do not come to know God through some sort of private revelation but rather through the actions of his Son, Jesus. What did Jesus do? He brought sight to the blind, liberation to prisoners, healing to the sick, joy and hope to those in despair, forgiveness to sinners, and new life to all. As followers of Jesus, we follow in his footsteps, making God known to others through action. Holy Communion is not a call to retreat into seclusion with God but is rather a call to action. In his letter, St. James challenges us to "be doers of the word, and not merely hearers" (James 1:22).

Receiving the body and blood of Jesus Christ allows us to express our commitment to be doers of the word. Receiving the body of Christ under the appearance of bread is an expression of our unity with all of God's people since we believe that, through baptism, we become members of Christ's mystical body. Receiving the precious Blood from the cup is an expression of our commitment to the mission of the church. In the Garden of Gethsemane, Jesus was tempted to abandon his commitment: "remove this cup from me" (Luke 22:42). Jesus, however, remained committed to his Father's will. In the same way, our drinking from the cup is a sign of our commitment to do the will of God. Receiving communion on Sunday is an expression of our commitment to enter into communion with our brothers and sisters each and every day. Within a matter of minutes after receiving communion, we will be sent forth to begin doing the work of loving God by loving our neighbors in our daily lives. The Eucharist is not a fueling station to pump us up for doing the Lord's work in a world that will drain us. Rather, it is a call to embrace humanity as God does: encouraging people to live as God's children and challenging them when they fall short. Regular reception of Holy Communion conditions us to recognize God's presence revealed in the world and to remember that he sent his only Son to become one of us.

The Communion Rite draws to a close with a prayer—the Prayer after Communion—which, as we should be expecting now, points us toward the exits and signals the fact that our work is just beginning.

The Other Six Days of the Week

With regard to daily life, Holy Communion invites and challenges us to

- recognize that God alone is the source of our fulfillment;

- admit our dependence on God;

- identify ways in which we sometimes strive to seek fulfillment;

- identify potential addictions in our lives;

- get in touch with our deepest hopes and desires and ask God to fulfill them;

- channel our desires so that they are fulfilled in healthy ways;

- recognize and overcome temptation;

- recognize the presence of Jesus in ourselves and in all those we meet;

- commit ourselves to the mission of the church;

- affirm goodness in all of God's creation, and challenge others to live as brothers and sisters.

■ ■ ■

Surely, this commandment that I am commanding you today is not too hard for you, nor is it too far away. It is not in heaven, that you should say, "Who will go up to heaven for us, and get it for us so that we may hear it and observe it?" Neither is it beyond the sea, that you should say, "Who will cross to the other side of the sea for us, and get it for us so that we may hear it and observe it?" No, the word is very near to you; it is in your mouth and in your heart for you to observe.

Deuteronomy 30:11–14

13

Go!

The Concluding Rites

Chicago Bulls basketball fans fondly recall the six NBA championships won by the Bulls during the Michael Jordan/Scottie Pippen era of the 1990s. After Michael Jordan retired (the first time!), it was clear that this was now "Scottie's team." Indeed, Scottie Pippen grabbed the bull by the horns (pun intended) and led the team through the season and toward the playoffs. In one particular game, however, Scottie showed a different side of himself. The game was tied with 1.8 seconds on the clock, and the Bulls had the ball. The team gathered during a time-out to find out the plan for the winning shot, everybody assuming the ball would go to Scottie. Coach Phil Jackson, however, designed a play that called for Toni Kukoc to take the shot. Scottie was livid, and he let it be known. Coach Jackson did not back down. Scottie then proceeded to take himself out of the game, choosing instead to sit on the bench and sulk. Play resumed, and Toni Kukoc scored the winning shot. Scottie, the team leader, had some explaining to do. He had put himself before the team, an action that damaged his reputation for the rest of his career. Just 1.8 seconds. That's all it took. (JSP)

You've probably figured out where we're going with this story. Scottie Pippen left before the game was over. Team members don't do that. Unfortunately, as we approach the end of the Mass, too many among us pull a "Scottie": We leave early, before the final blessing. Perhaps we figure that we've received communion, so we "got what we came for." Perhaps we're in a hurry to get to the parking lot before it crowds up too much or to get to the bakery before the line gets too long. Whatever the reason, we are tempted to leave before the final blessing and dismissal. So, what's the big deal?

When we gather for the Eucharist, we are led to the altar by the cross in the opening procession. We gather as a body and, throughout the Mass, by virtue of our actions and shared responses, are formed into the Body of Christ. We are about to be sent forth, not as lone rangers, but as a community of faith, unified in Christ Jesus. To leave early is to separate ourselves from the community. In essence, we start our own procession, separate from the procession that will be led once again by the cross of Jesus, this time away from the altar and back into the world. We are putting ourselves ahead of the team. To wait for the blessing, the dismissal, and for the cross of Jesus to lead us out of church in the closing procession is one final gesture on our part to express bodily what we expressed earlier in the creed: that we are "one holy, catholic, and apostolic church."

We are *one,* meaning that we are unified. We leave church in a unified manner to express this more profoundly.

We are *holy,* meaning that we are followers of the one and only Holy One: God. We leave church led by the cross, the symbol of God's holiness.

We are *catholic,* meaning that we are universal and are sent to proclaim the Good News to all nations. We leave church in a manner reminiscent of an army being sent on a mission.

We are *apostolic,* meaning not only that we trace our roots to the apostles, but also that we are sent, commissioned by Jesus to proclaim his word. We leave the church in a way that expresses our apostolic mission; we are sent forth to do the work of the apostles.

A few seconds can make a world of difference. Just ask Scottie Pippen. The Concluding Rites take only a few seconds, and yet these few seconds set the tone for how we are to go forth to live the Mass each day of our lives. So what happens in these brief moments that make up the Concluding Rites? We begin with the same formal exchange with which we began the Mass, prepared to receive the gospel, and entered into the Eucharistic Prayer:

Priest: The Lord be with you.

People: And with your spirit.

The presence of this exchange reminds us once again that we are about to embark upon a profound task. To leave before this exchange is to minimize the importance of the task at hand. What follows this exchange is an action that states very clearly whose mission it is upon which we are about to embark; we are given God's blessing. A blessing is a sign of approval and affirmation. Some people wait their entire lives hoping and praying for a blessing from their parents, some sign that shows that they approve and affirm their child for who he or she is. Many of us are lucky to receive such blessings throughout life. Others, sadly, are not. At Mass, we are privileged to receive this abundant blessing before we are sent forth.

> Priest: May Almighty God bless you
> the Father, the Son, and the Holy Spirit.

> People: Amen.

This blessing can be thought of as the moment in which we receive our credentials. Think about it. When an ambassador is sent to visit a foreign dignitary, the first thing he or she does is present a portfolio. This is an explicit way for ambassadors to express the fact that they are not speaking or acting in their own name and on their own behalf but in the name of the country and the leader who sent them. The final blessing of the Mass makes it clear that we are being sent forth, not in our own name, but in the name of the Holy Trinity—Father, Son, and Holy Spirit. St. Paul said that each of us is called to be an ambassador for Christ. The final blessing of the Mass is the moment in which we receive our credentials. To leave before this blessing is to suggest that we are operating in our own name, following our own agenda. To wait these precious few seconds is to completely reverse the meaning of our exit from the building. Now, armed with God's blessing—

our credentials that make us ambassadors for Christ—we are commanded to go forth and to begin our mission.

I experienced one of those a-ha moments while attending Mass during vacation in a small town on the coast of Maine. The celebrant was an older priest with features right out of a Winslow Homer painting, as craggy as the coastline itself. His style was warm and inviting, and I instantly felt good being there. After communion, I marveled that no one in the congregation moved to leave early. As the priest looked us all in the eye and said, "Go in peace," he reached down and scooped up an unsuspecting child no more than two years old and placed her on his left shoulder, making them look like an old holy card of St. Christopher and the child Jesus. My response of "Thanks be to God" was more than a happy exclamation celebrating the end of the liturgy. It was a personal clarion call for me to take what I had just learned from this wise old priest and share it with my own congregation and to become more like him as a celebrant, not doing Mass in the same old way. The congregation was beaming along with me as the priest processed out with the child during the triumphant recessional hymn. After he returned the nonplussed child to her proud parents, everyone waited patiently to shake his hand. Lest I paint too idyllic a picture, it must be noted that one of the reasons no one left Mass early was that the usher had locked the parking lot gate and only now, after everyone had exited the church, did he unlock it so people could leave. (DJG)

This simple recollection serves two purposes. One, it reminds us to retain our sense of humor when speaking about the Mass; it's easier to lift up our hearts when we are lighthearted! Second, and most important for our purposes in this book, it draws our attention to a part of the Mass that is easily overlooked: the very end. Recall that we began our exploration of the Mass in this book by looking ahead to the end of the Mass. We've come full circle now as we once again explore the Concluding Rites of the Mass. Everything else we do, say, pray—indeed, all the gestures, music, responses, and moments of silence—lead us inexorably to this moment when we are told to "go!" And because we are nurtured by the presence of our living God both in the words of Scripture and in the sacrament of the Eucharist, because we ask for and receive forgiveness in the Penitential Act, because we are challenged by the insights presented in the homily, because we bring our needs and hopes to the altar to be offered up in sacrifice to our God, and because we reach out in peace to one another in the community that has gathered, we are now given a mandate: "Go in peace." Just what do these powerful words mean, and how do we go about accomplishing this directive?

When we "go in peace," we go with a plan of action, with a sense of mission and direction. We go also with God's approval, as ambassadors of the gospel. Through the Concluding Rites, we receive our "marching orders" to carry out the work of the gospel and fulfill our baptismal commitment. When we are dismissed—sent forth—from the Mass, the priest or deacon does so with any of the following commands:

Go forth, the mass is ended.

Go and announce the Gospel of the Lord.

Go in peace, glorifying the Lord by your life.

Go in peace.

As is always the case in these prayerful exchanges during the Mass, the assembly gets the last word!

People: "Thanks be to God."

We are thankful to be considered worthy of being sent forth to do God's work in God's own name. We are thankful to know that we have a key part to play in God's game plan. Of course, in life, things do not always go exactly according to plan. Life does not follow a script. Even so, it is good to know that we Catholics are equipped with a basic plan as we leave the church. As Louis Pasteur, the famous chemist, biologist, and researcher, once said, "Chance favors the prepared mind."

When we are sent forth in the Concluding Rites of the Mass, we are not sent with a script, a lesson plan, a blueprint, or a playbook. Yet we are sent with a basic plan. The Concluding Rites, because of their brevity, leave a lot to the imagination. We are blessed and sent forth to get to work. While the Mass sends us in a general direction, it is up to us to put God's word into action day in and day out. The church provides a great deal of help and guidance to do this work effectively. Through *catechesis,* or the learning of our faith tradition, we acquire the knowledge and skills we need to live as disciples of Christ in the world. First and foremost, the Church equips us with some basic formulas of our faith that guide our thoughts and actions, namely, the Ten Commandments and the corporal and spiritual works of mercy.

The Ten Commandments

We tend to think of the Ten Commandments as prohibitions that tell us what not to do. However, the commandments are meant to guide us to make choices that allow us to live as God wants us to live. The first three commandments tell us how to love God. The remaining seven commandments show us how to love others. Here we list the Ten Commandments, explaining where they are supported through the liturgy of the Mass.

- I am the LORD your God: you shall not have strange gods before me. The Profession of Faith teaches us to place our trust in God alone. The Scripture readings teach us how God alone is our salvation. Holy Communion teaches us that God alone sustains us and that we should place God first above all things. Most important, the Mass as a whole teaches us to worship God alone.

- You shall not take the name of the LORD your God in vain. The Penitential Act teaches us to be pure in our words. The Scripture readings teach us why God's name is so great. The Gloria, the Gospel Acclamation, the Holy, Holy, Holy, the Eucharistic

Prayer, and the songs sung during the Mass teach us to respect, praise, and honor God's name and everything God stands for. The sign of the cross at the beginning and end of the Mass teaches us to respect God's name and to speak and act in God's name and in a manner that is worthy of God's name. The Mass as a whole teaches us to respect the sacred, which God's name represents.

- Remember to keep holy the LORD's day. The Introductory Rites teach us that it is important to gather together as a community in the name of the Lord. The Eucharistic Prayer teaches us to recall how God has brought salvation to his people and to respond by keeping the covenant, which is expressed by keeping the Sabbath. The Scripture readings help us to recall the wonderful things that God has done and to respond in praise, thanksgiving, and a life of holiness, all of which are the goal of the Lord's Day. The Mass as a whole teaches us that the resurrection of Jesus, which occurred on the first day of the week, is to be celebrated every day of our lives.

- Honor your father and your mother. The Scripture readings teach us to love our neighbor, a command that begins at home. The Prayer of the Faithful teaches us to assume responsibility as citizens of earth and to show respect for leaders and those who govern and exercise authority over others. The Our Father teaches us to show love, care, and respect for our heavenly Father as well as for those whom God has entrusted with his authority, beginning with our earthly parents and extending to family members, elders, and all of those in positions of authority.

- You shall not kill. The Penitential Act teaches us to show love toward others in our thoughts, words, and actions. The Scripture readings teach us to show love and respect for all human life. The Profession of Faith teaches us that God is the maker of all human life. The Prayer of the Faithful teaches us to show respect for the dead and to defend the dignity and lives of all people. The sign of peace teaches us to avoid anger and hatred, and to share the peace of Christ with others.

- You shall not commit adultery. The Penitential Act teaches us to be pure in our thoughts. The Profession of Faith reminds us that our bodies are created in the image of God and that the dignity of the human body is heightened by the fact that God took on human flesh through Jesus. The Lord's Prayer teaches us to resist temptation. Holy Communion teaches us that our bodies are the temple of the living God, our desires can be fulfilled only by God, and our communion with others is lived out through faithful relationships.

- You shall not steal. The creed teaches us that God created all things for all people. The Prayer of the

Faithful teaches us to show concern for the needs of the poor and vulnerable. The Presentation of the Gifts teaches us to be grateful for what we have and to live as stewards who show concern and respect for the rights and property of others, who are committed to fairness, who are generous in giving to those in need, and who respect the gifts of creation that God has given to us.

- You shall not bear false witness against your neighbor. The Penitential Act teaches us to be people of honesty and truth. The Scripture readings teach us that God is truth and that we are called to live in truth. The homily teaches us how to bear witness to the truth. The Profession of Faith teaches us to be committed to the truth. The Lord's Prayer teaches us to give others the benefit of the doubt by praying for their forgiveness.

- You shall not covet your neighbor's wife. The Penitential Act teaches us to be pure in our thoughts and to be humble, both of which lead to modesty. Holy Communion teaches us that God alone can fulfill our desires; communion also teaches us to see others as God sees them.

- You shall not covet your neighbor's goods. The Penitential Act teaches us humility, which is the opposite of the pride that often leads to envy. The Presentation of the Gifts teaches us to practice the spirit of poverty by being detached from material possessions and generous toward others. The Lord's Prayer teaches us to be satisfied with our daily bread, to avoid temptation, and to attribute all power and glory to God. Holy Communion teaches us to allow Jesus to satisfy our spiritual appetite.

The Corporal and Spiritual Works of Mercy

We often wonder what will happen when we die and come face-to-face with Jesus for our final judgment. Jesus actually made it quite clear what the criteria for our final judgment will be when he told the parable of the Last Judgment:

[Jesus said,] "I was hungry and you gave me food, I was thirsty and you gave me something to drink, I was a stranger and you welcomed me, I was naked and you gave me clothing, I was sick and you took care of me, I was in prison and you visited me." (Matthew 25:35–36)

These acts form the basis of what we have come to know as the corporal works of mercy. The corporal works of mercy are kind acts by which we help our neighbors with their everyday material and physical needs. The church also gives us works of mercy that tend to the emotional and spiritual needs of people. These are called the spiritual works of mercy. The key to all of the works of mercy is that these are not the sorts of actions that happen by accident. In order for them to happen, we need to be proactive. When we think about what it is we are to do when we are sent forth from Mass, the corporal and spiritual works of mercy can act as guides for our actions.

The Corporal Works of Mercy

- feeding the hungry

- sheltering the homeless

- clothing the naked

- visiting the sick and imprisoned

- giving alms to the poor

- burying the dead

The Spiritual Works of Mercy

- instructing

- advising

- consoling

- comforting

- forgiving

- bearing wrongs patiently

- praying for the living and the dead

In addition to teaching us *what* we are to do in the name of Jesus, the Church also teaches us *how* we are to go about doing these things. Followers of Jesus are to possess an attitude that pervades our actions. Through the gifts of the Holy Spirit, the fruit of the Holy Spirit, and the seven virtues, we develop the holy character from which good actions come.

The Gifts of the Holy Spirit

Today, it is common for people to rely on lawyers for many things. In our society, understanding laws has become increasingly complex. Lawyers help by providing legal guidance and expertise in situations that are too challenging for us to face on our own. We sometimes refer to lawyers with the title *counselor.* Jesus wisely gave us a "counselor" to assist us in becoming disciples, namely, the Holy Spirit. Since living as a disciple of Jesus can be challenging, Jesus' Spirit remains with us and provides the following gifts to help us when we are sent forth to live out our calling.

Wisdom. Wisdom enables us to see life from God's point of view and to recognize the real value of persons, events, and things. Wisdom keeps us from foolishly judging only by appearances.

Understanding. Understanding gives us insight into the truths of the faith and of being disciples of Jesus. It helps us make good choices in our relationships with God and others. Understanding grows through prayer and the reading of Scripture and through active listening.

Counsel (Right Judgment). The gift of counsel helps us give advice, seek advice, and be open to the advice of others. With the help of this gift, we are able to help others with their problems without judging them.

Fortitude. The gift of fortitude enables us to stand up for our beliefs, to do what is right in the face of difficulties, and to endure suffering with faith. This courage helps us not only to undertake challenging tasks in the service of our faith but also to be faithful in our everyday lives. It takes strength and courage to live a good Christian life, even when no one notices our efforts.

Knowledge. The gift of knowledge helps us to know what God asks of us and how we should respond. We come to know God, ourselves, and the real value of things through our experiences. This gift also helps us to recognize temptations for what they are and turn to God for help.

Fear of the Lord. The gift of fear of the Lord is not about being afraid but about having a sense of wonder and awe at the greatness of God and our dependence on him. It leads us to marvel at God's incredible love for us.

Piety (Reverence). Reverence is a gift that helps us love and worship God. It calls us to be faithful in our relationships with God and others. Reverence also helps us to be respectful and generous toward others and, like St. Francis of Assisi, toward all of God's creation.

The Fruits of the Holy Spirit

Wind is invisible. So how do we know it exists? We see and feel its effects. We see trees, plants, and flowers swaying, and we know that the wind is at work. In the same way, we recognize the presence of the Holy Spirit by the effects the Spirit has on people. People who are filled with the Holy Spirit show the effects of the Spirit's presence in their lives. We call these effects the fruits of the Holy Spirit. When Christians exemplify the fruits of the Holy Spirit, they attract other people to want to become disciples themselves. In fact, a great church father of the third century, Tertullian, quoted non-Christians as saying about Jesus' followers, "See how they love one another." Jesus himself told his disciples, "By this everyone will know that you are my disciples, if you have love for one another" (John 13:35). As we are sent forth to do the work of the gospel, we do so in a manner that expresses qualities known as the fruits of the Holy Spirit.

Love. Another word for love is *charity,* shown in selfless service to others by words and actions. Charity is a sign that we love God and that we love others as Jesus loves us. "Remember, Lord, your Church, spread throughout the world, and bring her to the fullness of charity" (Eucharistic Prayer II).

Faithfulness. We need to keep our promises. We are faithful when we show loyalty to God and to those to whom we have committed ourselves. Faithful people are dependable, trustworthy, and obedient. "May he help us by his grace to remain faithful to the Spirit we have received" (Rite for the Blessing and Sprinkling of Water).

Joy. Joy is deep and constant gladness in the Lord that circumstances cannot destroy. It comes from a good relationship with God and others—a relationship of genuine love. "There we hope to enjoy for ever the fullness of your glory" (Eucharistic Prayer III).

Modesty. Modesty is moderation in all our actions, especially our conversations and external behavior. Modesty is a sign that we give credit to God for our talents and successes. "With humble spirit and contrite heart may we be accepted by you, O Lord, and may our sacrifice in your sight this day be pleasing to you, Lord God" (Preparation of the Altar).

Kindness. Kindness is shown by generous acts of service. Kind people are compassionate and considerate, always striving to see the best in others. "Help us imitate you in your kindness" (Preface III of Lent).

Goodness. This fruit of the Spirit flows from God's great love. It is a sign that we love all people without exception. "For in goodness you created man" (Common Preface II).

Peace. Jesus said to his disciples on Easter morning, "Peace be with you" (John 20:21). A disciple faithful to God's will is serene, not overly anxious or upset. Peace comes from knowing that all will work out well because God is with us. "Peace I leave you, my peace I give you" (Sign of Peace).

Patience. Patience is love that is willing to endure life's suffering, difficulties, and routines. It means not giving up in difficult situations. It keeps us from being overwhelmed by life. "May he give you integrity in the faith, endurance in hope, and perseverance in charity, with holy patience to the end" (Solemn Blessing I, 3).

Self-control. We can discipline our physical and emotional desires by being modest and respectful of others. With self-control we can be in charge of our emotions and desires instead of the other way around. "And lead us not into temptation, but deliver us from evil" (the Lord's Prayer).

Chastity. Chastity is the integration of our physical sexuality with our spiritual nature. All people, married and single, are called to practice chastity "so that the human race may become holy, just as you yourself are holy" (Eucharistic Prayer for Reconciliation I).

Generosity. Generosity is a willingness to give, even at a cost to ourselves. It expresses concern for meeting the needs of others, even if it means sacrificing something of our own. "And that we might live no longer for ourselves" (Eucharistic Prayer IV).

Gentleness. Strength tempered by love leads us to be gentle, peaceful, and gracious. A gentle person has the power to forgive instead of getting angry. "Graciously grant that, following his example, we may always display the gentleness of your charity in the service of our neighbor" (Collect Prayer, St. Francis de Sales).

The Virtues

In his book *The 7 Habits of Highly Effective People*, Stephen R. Covey focuses on seven principles, or habits, for success. While Covey's idea is a brilliant approach to solving personal and professional problems, the concept is not unique. For centuries, the church has taught seven habits, or principles, that are key to living as disciples of Jesus. These habits are called *"virtues."* They can be referred to as habits because they need to be used; they can be lost if they are neglected. As we go forth from Mass to glorify the Lord with our lives, we can carry out our mission effectively if we rely on the following habits or virtues. The first three virtues are called *theological* virtues, because they come from God and lead to God. The remaining four—the *cardinal* virtues—are human virtues, acquired by education and good actions. They are named for the Latin word for "hinge" (*cardo*), meaning "that on which other things depend."

Like playing the piano, being a good friend, playing sports, or anything else worthwhile, these virtues take time and effort to develop. But through practice they can become a natural part of our lives. Too often, the phrase "practicing Catholic" is defined solely by attendance at Mass on Sunday. The Concluding Rites, however, remind us that we are to practice our faith day in and day out in the same way that a doctor practices medicine each day. By focusing on these responsibilities and the manner in which we carry them out, we can commit ourselves to being "practicing Catholics" not only on Sunday but always. Here are the seven virtues, the first three being the theological virtues and the last four being the cardinal virtues.

Faith. Faith, God's gift to us, is the ability to believe in God and give our lives to him. It makes us able to trust God completely and to accept all that God has revealed and taught us. "As you run the race of this present life, may he make you firm in faith . . ." (Solemn Blessing for Advent).

Hope. Hope is closely related to faith. It is the desire for all the good things God has planned for us. Hope gives us confidence that God will always be with us and that we will live with God forever in heaven. We trust in God who in turn trusts us. "There we hope to enjoy for ever the fullness of your glory . . ." (Eucharistic Prayer III).

Charity. Charity leads us to love God above all things and our neighbors as ourselves. This love involves more than just feelings; it is the way we think about God and act toward him. Charity brings all the virtues together in perfect harmony. "Now faith, hope, and love abide," St. Paul writes in 1 Corinthians 13:13, "and the greatest of these is love." "May he turn your steps toward himself and show you the path of charity. . ." (Solemn Blessing, Ordinary Time III).

Prudence. Prudence helps us to decide what is good and then choose to do it. It leads us to stop and think before we act so that when we act, we do so with a level head. "Deliver us, Lord, we pray, from every evil" (embolism after the Lord's Prayer).

Justice. Justice leads us to respect the rights of others and to give them what is rightfully theirs. The just person considers the needs of others and always tries to be fair. "And may your

Church stand as a living witness to truth and freedom, to peace and justice . . ." (Eucharistic Prayer for Use in Masses for Various Needs IV).

Fortitude. Fortitude is the courage to do what is right, even when it is very difficult. It provides the strength to resist the temptations we face. "And that your saving mysteries may be fulfilled, their great examples lend us courage . . ." (Preface II of Saints).

Temperance. Temperance helps us balance what we want with what we need. It helps us moderate our desires for enjoyment and builds self-control. "That they may remain faithful in holiness of life and, having enough for their needs in this world . . ." (Prayers over the People, 19).

When I was working as a pastoral associate and director of religious education at a Chicago parish, I would occasionally encounter parishioners who wanted to talk about their careers. Typically, they were people who were hungry for spiritual fulfillment and were experiencing great frustration with their jobs. They would say to me things like, "I wish I had your job. It must be great to feel so close to God, to be able to do God's work every day, to spend so much time in the church." Some would even ask for information about moving into a career in ministry. Part of me was excited to think that someone wanted to enter the ministry. Another part of me wanted to throttle them and say, "Are you crazy?" Little did they realize that while I enjoyed my ministry, I encountered the same frustrations on the job that they did: bosses and coworkers who could be difficult, tasks that often seemed tedious, "customers" who were never satisfied, long hours and low pay, and so on. I could not fathom the notion that somehow, by working for the church, I was seen as a better disciple of Christ than those who didn't. The fact is, the vast majority of people do not and will not ever work for the church. Somehow, unfortunately, we seem to have failed to communicate to people that God wants us to live up to our baptismal promises in our daily lives . . . not only in a church building or on parish grounds. (JSP)

An ancient Buddhist story tells of a novice asking a monk about how his life has changed as a result of achieving enlightenment. The monk responds by saying, "Before enlightenment, I chopped wood and carried water. After enlightenment, I chopped wood and carried water."

When we come to embrace our baptism, our lives change. When we receive the Eucharist each Sunday at Mass, we are changed. However, that change is not measured by how much time we spend in the church building or on the parish grounds. Nor is that change necessarily related to our daily activities. The change is more about doing things for a new and different reason, with a new and different approach, and from a new and different source.

Although Ebenezer Scrooge is a fictional character, do you think he quit his job, sold the business, and became a missionary after his conversion? No doubt he continued to run the Scrooge and Marley counting house, employ Bob Cratchit, and trade in various markets. What changed was why he did what he did and how he did it. While his conversion was certainly spiritual, it likely did not turn him into a "religious" or pious person who dropped "alleluias" and "amens" into every sentence.

When we leave the church after Mass, more deeply aware of our baptismal call to live as disciples of Christ, we need not think that we have to change jobs or speak more religiously on the job. Martin Luther King Jr. emphasized that it is in our everyday lives that we live out our true calling: "If it falls to your lot to be a street sweeper, sweep streets like Michelangelo painted pictures, sweep streets like Beethoven composed music, sweep streets like Leontyne Price sings before the Metropolitan Opera. Sweep streets like Shakespeare wrote poetry. Sweep streets so well that all the hosts of heaven and earth will have to pause to say: Here lived a great street sweeper who swept his job well."

In his book *Spirituality at Work*, author Gregory F. A. Pierce tells us that our spirituality "can be practiced right in the midst of our daily activities and that it is more a matter of awareness than of pious practices." He explains that some people think that to be disciples of Jesus means to "get yourself noticed and then to convert others or proselytize them to join your particular sect or denomination." Pierce describes Catholic evangelization as "more about actions than about words. It does not need to clothe itself in religious language to be effective." St. Ignatius of Loyola encouraged his followers to spread the faith with subtlety: "Whenever we wish to win someone over and engage him in the greater service of God our Lord, we should . . . enter his door with him, but we come out our own" *(How to Deal and Converse with Others in the Lord, Selected Letters of St. Ignatius of Loyola)*.

Some years ago, my mom was named the woman of the year by her parish and was invited to receive the award at a luncheon at which a couple of dozen parishes would be bestowing the same honor upon one of their own. Along with a number of my brothers and sisters, I attended and enjoyed a wonderful celebration that my mom and all the other women deeply deserved. As they were reading the short biographies of each of the women coming forward, I noticed something very intriguing. Not to take away from any of the awardees (especially my mom), but I realized that of all the twenty-five or so honorees, all but one were involved in ministries that directly served the parish itself. In other words, only one of the women was involved in ministries that reached out into the "secular" world. This particular honoree was involved in outreach to women in prison, helping them to make recordings of themselves reading stories so their children could hear their mother's voice. She was also involved in airport ministry, offering hospitality to travelers, as well as a number of other activities that reached out to people in need. All the other women were being honored for "churchy" involvements: serving as lectors, ministers of communion, sacristans; decorating the sanctuary; changing the water in the holy-water receptacles; cleaning the church; washing and ironing the purificators; and so on. While all these selfless women are to be admired, I had to wonder how we arrived at the point of thinking that the most admirable way to live out one's faith somehow involved spending more of our personal time in the church building! (JSP)

What does all this mean in terms of how we are to live out the mandate to "go in peace"? When Jesus tells us to "do this in memory of me," what is it that he wants us to do? For most of us, we conclude that we should be more spiritual people. Yet what does it mean to be spiritual? What is spirituality? If you were to ask most people to create a pie chart showing what proportion of their lives is dedicated to spiritual pursuits, many people would devote a tiny sliver, indicating the time they spent in church, in prayer, reading Scripture, or participating in a church activity or ministry. The rest of the pie is made up of work, family, recreation, sleep, and so on. Unfortunately, because of our misunderstanding of spirituality, we tend to think that the goal is to increase that "spiritual" slice of the pie by increasing the amount of time devoted to going to church, praying, reading Scripture, and being involved in church activities. Spirituality, however, is not about increasing a slice of the pie devoted to church activities. It is about a way of looking at the whole pie— our entire lives—in relation to God. In his book *The Holy Longing*, Ronald Rolheiser describes spirituality as "finding the proper ways, disciplines, by which to both access . . . energy and contain it." He's not just talking about what we do with our energy when we are in church, praying, reading Scripture, or being involved in church activities. Spirituality is about what we are doing with our energy every moment of our lives. In other words, to be a spiritual person is to see the entire "pie" as spiritual. Like the two disciples on the road to Emmaus, our eyes can be opened so that we recognize the presence of Jesus walking in our midst on the road of life. That story teaches us that it is the breaking of the bread— the Eucharist—that leads to such an eye-opener.

Jesus was born in a barn, and yet for some reason we often seek him only in churches and monasteries. When Jesus proclaimed the kingdom of God, he didn't tell people that they could find it in the temple or in the synagogues. He said, "The kingdom of God has come near" (Mark 1:15), meaning that it is right in our midst. *The kingdom of God* is a phrase that describes the reality of God's will or rule in our lives. Simply put, God's will is our salvation. When Jesus says that "the kingdom of God has come near," he is telling us that salvation is all around us. The Eucharist opens our eyes to the reality of salvation above us, below us, in front of us, behind us, and all around us. As baptized followers of Jesus, we commit ourselves to revealing this reality to others.

This takes practice. Daily practice. That's what it means to be practicing Catholics. Think of how we learn to ride a bike. We don't practice riding a bike and then one day start riding the bike. We simply begin riding—poorly at first and then better as we continue to practice. In the same way, discipleship is not something that we practice for a while in preparation for beginning the "real thing." To be "practicing" Catholics means that we are attempting to do the work of the gospel each day. We may do it poorly at first, but we are doing it. There is no measure of success when it comes to discipleship. There is only faithfulness.

The Other Six Days of the Week

With regard to daily life, the Concluding Rites invite and challenge us to

- bring the good news of Jesus Christ into every aspect of our daily lives: home, work, play, family, friends, neighborhood, country, and world;

- live each day according to God's plan as revealed by Jesus;

- go about life in such a way as to attract others to Jesus;

- live out our baptismal callings;

- practice our Catholicism every day;

- see every aspect of life as spiritual.

■ ■ ■

Love proves itself by deeds, so how am I to show my love? Great deeds are forbidden me. The only way I can prove my love is by scattering flowers and these flowers are every little sacrifice, every glance and word, and the doing of the least actions for love.

St. Thérèse of Lisieux, *The Little Way*

14

Living the Mass

We Are Not Alone

Most of us had been glued to our television sets all day. It was a September 11 we would never forget. At the parish, we posted an announcement on our Web site that a special Mass would be celebrated that evening at 7:00 p.m. We unlocked the church for people to come in and pray, and we put signs all over the neighborhood announcing the Mass. Not surprisingly, the church filled beyond capacity for the liturgy. It was quiet and sad. People were deep in prayer. After Mass was over, I announced that church would remain open as long as people wanted to be there. I stood at the doors as the closing hymn ended. What happened next was an important moment in my understanding of what liturgy means, what church means, and what community means. No one got up to leave. People sat and knelt in silent prayer for a significant period of time. Then they started to leave their pews slowly. But still they remained in church talking with one another, embracing, holding hands. They were slowly coming to understand that their lives had been changed, and they were coming to grips with what this would mean to them as people of faith. I realized how important it was for us to come together and celebrate Mass. So many people thanked me for scheduling the Mass. And many of them repeated the same sentiments: "We knew you would have Mass tonight." "We knew we had to come to Mass tonight." "We knew St. Josaphat's would say the right thing to us." "We knew you wouldn't let us down." It was hard to end that liturgy with the words "Go in peace," but they may have been the most important words we heard throughout that long and terrible day. (DJG)

The task of living from day to day as disciples of Jesus Christ may seem quite daunting, and indeed it is. On some occasions, as on September 11, 2001, leaving the church to go out into the world can seem downright frightening. And yet our faith tells us that good will prevail. From the beginning of the book of Genesis to the end of the book of Revelation, we are taught that God's creation is good, that we are made in God's image, and that God continually makes all things new. Aware of our fears, however, Jesus assures us that we are not left to our own devices to carry out his mission. Jesus has given us his Holy Spirit, who teaches us, through the church, what it is that we are to do and how we are to do it:

The Advocate, the Holy Spirit, whom the Father will send in my name, will teach you everything, and remind you of all that I have said to you. (John 14:26)

Through the church, the Holy Spirit does indeed teach us and remind us of what Jesus told us. These teachings provide the tools we need to carry out our responsibilities as disciples of Christ who literally go in peace, glorifying the Lord with our lives. All these teachings suggest concrete ways to carry out the task of discipleship and the manner in which to do it. When we celebrate the Eucharist, we not only receive the strength, nourishment, and direction for carrying out this task—we actually begin the task. The word *liturgy*—another word for the Mass—comes from the Greek word *leitourgia,* meaning "the work of the people." In other words, the Mass is not a rehearsal or a warm-up for the work that follows; it is the place where we begin the work that we will continue as we leave. Now that we have gone through every part of the Mass, let's conclude by looking at some practical suggestions for how we can continue to do the work of the gospel after we leave the sanctuary and move about in our day-to-day lives at home and in the workplace. It is important to remember that we do not do any of these things to earn God's grace; we do them to *respond* to God's grace, which is given to us freely. The commitment each of us made in baptism to live as a disciple of Christ is carried out mainly in the time we spend at work and at home, which is the majority of our time. That is where the Eucharist (the presence of Jesus) is needed most and where we are called to participate in Jesus' ministry as *priest, prophet,* and *king.*

The Mass in Summary

In the **Introductory Rites** of the Mass we begin the work of leaving behind individualism and entering into community.

Below are some suggestions for how to continue this work during the other six days of the week.

- Acknowledge the presence of others through a warm smile, a nod of the head, or a simple greeting.

- Extend hospitality to those we encounter at work, on the street, and in our homes and communities.

- Focus on the needs of others.

- Call or drop in on a friend or family member for no particular reason.

- Reach out and bring hope to those who are lonely (especially at mealtimes).

- Recognize the dignity of others who are created in the image of God.

- Speak out on behalf of those who are marginalized.

- Focus on what we have in common with others rather than on our differences.

- Be patient and respectful toward others in public places, especially while driving or taking public transportation.

- Resist the urge to be mean-spirited when using social media.

In the **Penitential Act** of the Mass we begin the work of developing a sense of humility. Below are some suggestions for how to continue this work during the other six days of the week.

- Do work quietly behind the scenes.

- Direct praise toward others instead of seeking it for ourselves.

- Compliment coworkers on their efforts.

- Discreetly give credit to God when congratulated for successes.

- Speak out on behalf of those in need who are too humble to draw attention to themselves.

- Do acts of kindness for others without calling attention to ourselves.

- Help others to succeed.

- Forgive others as God forgives us.

- Speak respectfully in public (or refrain from speaking) of someone we have difficulty with.

- Refrain from passing judgment on others.

- Acknowledge and accept our own imperfections.

- Review our days and identify times we may have been less than what God wants us to be.

- Take constructive criticism to heart.

- Spend time with people who keep our heads from getting too big.

- Remember how good God has been to us even though we've done nothing to earn it.

In the **Liturgy of the Word,** we begin the work of recognizing the extraordinary context in which our lives take place so that we can share that good news with others. Below are some suggestions for how to continue this work during the other six days of the week.

- Recall a word or phrase (write it on a sticky note and place it on a mirror, computer monitor, or refrigerator) from the Scripture readings or homily, using it to remind us to put the message of God's word into action in concrete ways each day.

- Recognize God's voice in the experiences of each day.

- Recognize all people as part of the story of our salvation.

- Look more closely for evidence of God's loving presence in the everyday.

- Help others connect their joys and struggles to a larger story.

- Assure those in despair that they can find hope by placing their lives in the context of God's love.

- Offer alternative ways to view things, especially when people are voicing thoughts and opinions contrary to the gospel.

- Speak and act with authority, suggesting and showing practical ways to act upon gospel values in everyday life.

- Speak and act as witnesses to God's saving power.

- Live with an appreciation for the past, acceptance of the present, and hope for the future.

- Take some personal time to reflect, study, and become more familiar with God's word by reading Scripture and other inspirational literature.

- Keep a Bible handy, and read it or pray with it often.

- Look for comparisons and connections between our daily experiences and Scripture.

- Be open to the transformation that comes from placing God's word at the center of our lives and seeing things in new ways.

In the **Profession of Faith,** we begin the work of deepening our trust in God. Below are some suggestions for how to continue this work during the other six days of the week.

- Trust coworkers to carry out their tasks and fulfill their roles; trust family members and friends with responsibilities.

- Encourage coworkers, family members, and friends to trust that their honest efforts are worthwhile and will bear fruit.

- Live with confidence, conviction, and courage.

- Discreetly articulate our trust in God, especially in difficult situations.

- Live without fear, helping to dispel fear from the lives of others.

- Bring hope to others by encouraging them to trust in difficult situations.

- Allow others to trust in us.

- Restore trust by reaching out across divides (racial, economic, religious, and so on) by doing acts of kindness without expecting anything in return and by keeping our promises and apologizing when we break them.

- Show respect for people with different religious beliefs, and speak openly and confidently with them about our beliefs.

- Act according to our beliefs and in a way that is fitting with the title *disciple.*

- Know and understand the words of our faith that can help us articulate what we believe about our relationship with God and the church.

- Respect all of God's creation and help others to recognize the divine presence in all people and in God's creation.

- Recognize the face of Jesus in all human beings, especially coworkers, family members, friends, customers, clients, competitors, and those we encounter on the train, on the bus, on the road, in parking lots, in malls, at supermarkets, and so on.

- Don't be easily swayed by naysayers.

In the **Prayer of the Faithful,** we begin the work of praying for the needs of ourselves, others, the church, and the world. Below are some suggestions for how to continue this work during the other six days of the week.

- Live with an awareness of our total dependence on God.

- Live with sensitivity to the needs of others, and pray as a response to those needs.

- Assure others in need that we are praying for them.

- Check on those who have asked us for prayers.

- Pray for the needs and the well-being of coworkers, family, and friends.

- Pray for and act on behalf of those who are oppressed and vulnerable.

- Pray for the energy, strength, and courage to tend to the needs of others.

- Bring all our needs, concerns, and desires to God.

- Invite others to pray for the needs of those who are oppressed and vulnerable.

- Practice awareness of God's wonderful deeds and respond by seeking his continuing grace at work, at home, and at play.

- Be ever mindful, compassionate, and responsive to the needs of the world and of our local communities.

- Reach out to those who are ill and to those who care for them.

- Console the families of those who have died.

In the **Presentation of the Gifts,** we begin the work of sharing our time, talent, and treasure with others and with God. Below are some suggestions for how to continue this work during the other six days of the week.

- Share time and creativity with our coworkers, clients, and customers to tend to their needs and be of assistance.

- Recognize that our time at work is an opportunity to cooperate in God's ongoing creative process and in his maintenance of creation.

- Recognize that the time and energy we spend at work and caring for our family and friends are opportunities for selfless giving and not infringements on our "own" time.

- Identify opportunities to share time and talent with organizations that rely on volunteerism, especially for those in need.

- Share our treasure, especially when our time is limited, to support charitable organizations.

- Determine an appropriate percentage of our income to give back to God through support of charitable causes, thankful for the opportunity to keep the rest for our own needs and for the needs of our families.

- Be truly present to people when they are speaking to us, especially our families, friends, and coworkers.

- Bring hope to those who feel ignored by paying attention to them and their needs. Balance time between work and family so that healthy relationships are maintained.

- Live, work, and play with a spirit of poverty (a sense of detachment from material goods); a spirit of obedience (a sense of accountability when it comes to how we spend our time) to our employers, coworkers, spouses, friends, and family members; and a spirit of chastity (a recognition of our giftedness and a commitment to share those gifts appropriately with others).

- Live as good stewards of God's creation.

- Practice random acts of generosity.

In the **Eucharistic Prayer,** we begin the work of living with gratitude, remembering God's great deeds, calling on God to "come through" for us, recognizing his presence in our midst, and offering our lives to God. Below are some suggestions for how to continue this work during the other six days of the week.

- Go out of our way to acknowledge the presence of others—neighbors, commuters, coworkers, family members, and friends—while also being fully present to others, especially those who feel isolated.

- Make a concerted effort to express thanks to others for their efforts, especially those that typically go unnoticed.

- Begin and end our days by giving thanks to God for all the ways we have been blessed.

- Bring Jesus' presence (his compassion, understanding, forgiveness, joy, and so forth) to others, especially to those who are lonely or in despair.

- Remind ourselves that it is God's great deeds that make it possible for us to find fullness of life.

- Call on God to "come through" for us and for others, especially in times of need.

- Begin each morning by offering our day and ourselves to God.

- Dedicate our work each day to God's glory.

- Strive to make our days at work and at home holy (set apart for God's purposes).

- Send a personal message (a handwritten note, an e-mail, a tweet, etc.) to a friend or a shut-in.

In the **Lord's Prayer,** we begin the work of letting go of our own will (our desire to control), opening up to the will of God, and declaring our dependence on him. Below are some suggestions for how to continue this work during the other six days of the week.

- Let go of our efforts to control the day's agenda at work and at home.

- Let go of our efforts to control other people, especially coworkers and family members.

- Show confidence toward others at work and at home based on our trust in God's will.

- Assure those in despair that God's will is one of mercy and compassion.

- Involve ourselves in efforts that seek to demonstrate that God wants justice and mercy, especially for the oppressed and vulnerable.

- Practice forgiveness of others.

- Seek forgiveness from others, especially at home and at work.

- Recognize true power as service to others, not being served by them.

- Do all things for the greater glory of God and to bring honor to God's name.

- Live with a childlike attitude, acknowledging that we are dependent on God.

- Discern God's will in all situations, knowing that it means living in right relationship with others.

In the **Sign of Peace,** we begin the work of living in peaceful relationships with our brothers and sisters. Below are some suggestions for how to continue this work during the other six days of the week.

- Be positive in our thoughts and comments.

- Strive to strengthen relationships in our homes and workplaces.

- Embrace people for who they are instead of try to change them.

- Silently pray that Christ's peace fills each person we meet and greet throughout our days.

- Let go of our own anxieties, and help to dispel the anxieties of others.

- Seek to bring out the best in others, and be less judgmental.

- Work for justice, which is the foundation of peace.

- Vote; attend community meetings; speak out respectfully and listen attentively.

In the **Communion Rite** we begin the work of living as if God alone sustains us and of recognizing God's presence in all people. Below are some suggestions for how to continue this work during the other six days of the week.

- Recognize the presence of Jesus in ourselves and in all of those we meet, especially coworkers, customers, clients, family members, friends, and those we encounter daily on the bus, the train, on the road, in malls, at grocery stores, and so on.

- Encourage family, friends, and coworkers to see God's goodness in others.

- Remind ourselves and others that even in the midst of loss, God's presence and grace continue to sustain us.

- Affirm goodness in the world.

- Challenge others to live as brothers and sisters.

- Recognize our communion with all people by standing in solidarity with those who are oppressed and vulnerable, "washing the feet" of others by offering simple acts of selfless service in our homes and workplaces, and bringing God's grace to those in need through our service to them.

- Acknowledge at the start of each day that God alone is the source of our fulfillment.

- Identify potential or existing addictions in our lives.

- Identify (especially at the end of the day) unhealthy ways in which we may have attempted to seek fulfillment.

- Get in touch with our deepest hopes and desires, asking God to fulfill them.

- Channel our desires so that they are fulfilled in healthy ways.

- Recognize temptation and work to overcome it.

- Bake or bring a loaf of bread to someone who is struggling.

In the **Concluding Rites,** we begin the work of living out our baptismal commitment to bring the gospel to the world. Below are some suggestions for how to continue this work during the other six days of the week.

- View every aspect of our lives—home, work, play, relationships—as spiritual, and seek to bring the good news of Jesus into each of these aspects.

- Remind ourselves that we go forth with God's approval (blessing).

- Practice our faith each and every day through our actions and through the manner in which we act.

- Remind ourselves each day of God's plan for us as revealed in the Scriptures proclaimed at Sunday Mass.

- Make a commitment to ongoing faith formation (catechesis), which helps us to identify what we are to do and how we are to do it as disciples of Christ.

An elderly nun had served for many years as the sacristan of the parish where I became pastor. She was used to doing things her way. I was close to forty years her junior. It was not surprising that we might disagree on how things should be done at the weekend liturgies. But it surprised me that it all came to a head so soon—my first weekend in the parish. In order to save the parish precious money on electricity, Sister would turn off all the lights in church right after the closing hymn was announced. That meant I walked down the aisle in the dark at that first Saturday evening Mass. Afterward, I told her to leave the lights on, that I would turn them off when I returned to the sacristy after the final Mass of the day. The next morning, Sunday, there were no problems after the first two Masses. The lights were left on. But after the final Mass, as I stood on the steps meeting people for the first time, not only did the lights go off when I wasn't paying attention, but Sister had also locked the church doors—with me still out on the steps. I turned to go back into church, and I was locked out. It was a masterful act of passive-aggressive behavior on her part, which left me embarrassed as the remaining parishioners laughed with me on the steps. As I walked around the gangway to the side entrance for which I had a key, one of the old-timers made a very wise statement: "We're the ones who belong out here after Mass. You belong in there." As pastor of less than a week I wasn't sure how he had meant it, so I wasn't sure how to respond. Likewise, I was distracted by Sister walking resolutely past me to the convent, not looking me in the eye, but with a victorious smile on her face. Upon reflection, I realized that the old-time parishioner had spoken with much wisdom. He recognized that his role took him into the world and that my role was to gather people together in church in order to send them forth into that world. That first weekend, I learned that the parishioners would teach me a lot before it was all over. (DJG)

The Mass is that privileged place where we hear Jesus' words, "Do this in memory of me," and are sent forth with God's blessing to practice our faith: "Go in peace, glorifying the Lord with your lives." Together, as priests and laypeople, we have much work to do. Transforming the world is no easy task. Luckily, we are not alone. . . . "Thanks be to God."

■ ■ ■

[Jesus said,] "Go therefore and make disciples of all nations, baptizing them in the name of the Father and of the Son and of the Holy Spirit, and teaching them to obey everything that I have commanded you. And remember, I am with you always, to the end of the age."

Matthew 28:19–20

Resources

Join in. Speak up. Help out!

Would you like to help yourself and the greater Catholic community by simply talking about Catholic life and faith? Would you like to help Loyola Press improve our publications? Would you be willing to share your thoughts and opinions with us in return for rewards and prizes? If so, please consider becoming one of our *special Loyola Press Advisors.*

Loyola Press Advisors is a unique online community of people willing to share with us their perspectives about Catholic life, spirituality, and faith. From time to time, registered advisors are invited to participate in brief online surveys and discussion groups. As a show of our gratitude for their service, we recognize advisors' time and efforts with *gift certificates, cash, and other prizes.* Membership is free and easy. We invite you, and readers like yourself, to join us by registering at **www.spiritedtalk.org**.

Your personal information gathered by spiritedtalk.org is stored in a protected, *confidential* database. Your information will never be sold to or shared with a third party! And SpiritedTalk.org is for research purposes only; at no time will we use the Web site or your membership to try to sell you anything.

Once you have registered at SpiritedTalk.org, every now and then you will be invited to participate in surveys—most take less than ten minutes to complete. Survey topics include your thoughts and ideas regarding the products and services you use in relation to Catholic life and spiritual growth.

You may also have the opportunity to evaluate new Loyola Press products and services before they are released for sale. Membership is voluntary; you may opt out at any time.

Please consider this opportunity to help Loyola Press improve our products and better serve you and the greater Catholic community.

We invite you to visit **www.SpiritedTalk.org**, take a look, and register today!

Also Available

by Fr. Dominic Grassi

Still Called by Name: Why I Love Being a Priest
ISBN-13: 978-0-8294-1715-9
ISBN-10: 0-8294-1715-X
5½" x 8½" Hardcover • 208 pages • $19.95

***Bumping into God: 35 Stories of Finding Grace in
Unexpected Places***
ISBN-13: 978-0-8294-1654-1
ISBN-10: 0-8294-1654-4
5" x 7" Paperback • 174 pages • $10.95

***Bumping into God Again: 35 More Stories of Finding Grace in
Unexpected Places***
ISBN-13: 978-0-8294-1648-0
ISBN-10: 0-8294-1648-X
5" x 7" Paperback • 200 pages • $10.95

***Bumping into God in the Kitchen: Savory Stories of Food,
Family, and Faith***
ISBN-13: 978-0-8294-1618-3
ISBN-10: 0-8294-1618-8
5" x 7" Paperback • 216 pages • $12.95

Available through your favorite bookstore or Web site, or
call **800.621.1008** or visit **www.loyolabooks.com** to order.

Also Available

by Joe Paprocki, D. Min.

The Catechist's Toolbox: How to Thrive as a Religious Education Teacher
ISBN-13: 978-0-8294-2451-5
ISBN-10: 0-8294-2451-2
7" x 9" Paperback • 148 pages • $9.95
Also available in Spanish!

A Well-Built Faith: A Catholic's Guide to Knowing and Sharing What We Believe
ISBN-13: 978-0-8294-2757-8
ISBN-10: 0-8294-2757-0
7" x 9" Paperback • 192 pages • $9.95

The Bible Blueprint: A Catholic's Guide to Understanding and Embracing God's Word
ISBN-13: 978-0-8294-2898-8
ISBN-10: 0-8294-2898-4
7" x 9" Paperback • 144 pages • $9.95

Practice Makes Catholic: Moving from a Learned Faith to a Lived Faith
ISBN-13: 978-0-8294-3322-7
ISBN-10: 0-8294-3322-8
7" x 9" Paperback • 208 pages • $9.95

Available through your favorite bookstore or Web site, or call **800.621.1008** or visit **www.loyolabooks.com** to order.